EDITED BY
SUNERA THOBANI

THE DEADLY INTERSECTIONS OF COVID-19

Race, States, Inequalities and Global Society

BRISTOL
UNIVERSITY
PRESS

First published in Great Britain in 2022 by

Bristol University Press
University of Bristol
1–9 Old Park Hill
Bristol
BS2 8BB
UK
t: +44 (0)117 374 6645
e: bup-info@bristol.ac.uk

Details of international sales and distribution partners are available at
bristoluniversitypress.co.uk

British Library Cataloguing in Publication Data
A catalogue record for this book is available from the British Library

ISBN 978-1-5292-2466-5 hardcover
ISBN 978-1-5292-2467-2 ePub
ISBN 978-1-5292-2468-9 ePdf

Cover design: blu inc
Front cover image: alamy.com/Jess Rodríguez
Bristol University Press and Policy Press use environmentally responsible
print partners.
Printed in Great Britain by CPI Group (UK) Ltd, Croydon, CR0 4YY

Contents

List of Figure and Tables

Notes on Contributors

Farida Akhter is a women's rights activist and founding Director of Policy Research Organization and the Women's Book Store in Bangladesh. She is a leading exponent of biodiversity-based ecological agriculture. She is campaigning against the harmful, unethical, deceptive and coercive introduction of GM crops in Bangladesh since the late 1990s by both raising awareness and demonstrating successful alternatives. She writes regularly for national daily newspapers in both Bangla and English, and spends most of her time working with farmers in the village, organizing farmers' rallies in Dhaka to draw the attention of policy makers, and coordinating press conferences to brief journalists on the issue. She also arranges workshops and trainings with researchers, NGOs, activists, women's groups and consumer groups on various issues related to health, food, agriculture and ecological lifestyles.

Radha D'Souza is Professor of Law, Development and Conflict Studies at the School of Law, University of Westminster where she chairs the Law, Development and Conflicts research group. Radha's research and writing straddles several disciplines and focuses on the Global South, law colonialism and neo-colonialism, history of imperialism in South Asia, and comparative theory and philosophy. She has written and published extensively on a range of subjects and issues concerning social and global justice. Her recent book *What's Wrong With Rights? Social Movements, Law and Liberal Imaginations* (Pluto, 2018) maps the transformations in the regime of international rights to the transformations in post-World War imperialism. She has written on activism and the security state, anti-colonial movements in South Asia, and on militarization and ethno-national conflicts in South Asia. Her current research focuses on corporations and international development. Radha is a critical scholar, social justice activist, barrister and writer from India.

Mengzhu Fu is a diasporic Chinese activist and doctoral student at York University, based between Tāmaki-Makaurau and Toronto. They have a background in migrant youth work and activism on issues of racism, gender-based violence, and Asian solidarity with Indigenous sovereignty movements primarily in Aotearoa (colonially known as 'New Zealand'). Their research focuses on Chinese diasporic solidarity with Indigenous movements in Aotearoa and Canada-occupied Turtle Island.

Jin Haritaworn is Associate Professor of Gender, Race and Environment at York University. They have authored various publications, including two books, numerous articles (in journals such as *GLQ, Society & Space* and *Sexualities*), and four co/edited collections (including *Queer Necropolitics*), which are widely read and taught on both sides of the Atlantic. Their latest book, *Queer Lovers and Hateful Others: Regenerating Violent Times and Places*, is on queer gentrification and criminalization, anti-Muslim racism and queer of colour kitchen tables in Berlin. Jin has made foundational contributions to several debates, including homonationalism, intersectionality, transnational sexuality studies, and queer of colour space and politics.

Sabiha Hussain is Professor and Director at Sarojini Naidu Centre for Women's Studies, Jamia Millia Islamia University, New Delhi. Before joining the Centre for Women's Studies, she worked as Associate Professor and Professor/Director in the Centre for Social Exclusion and Inclusive Policy under KR Narayanan Centre for Dalit and Minorities Studies, Jamia Millia Islamia. She worked as junior fellow (I & II) in the Centre for Women's Development Studies, New Delhi for more than a decade before coming to Jamia Millia Islamia. She obtained her MPhil and PhD from the Centre for the Study of Social

System, School of Social Sciences, Jawaharlal Nehru University. Apart from teaching she has been extensively engaged in research on gender issues and the problems faced by women in contemporary times. She has guided MPhil, Master's and PhD scholars. She has authored six books, including *Gender Inclusion in India: Challenges and Strategies* (2021), *Women and Livelihood: Assertion for Visibility: A Study of Home based Workers in Northern India* (2020), *Women in Higher Education* (2019), *Pervasive Exclusion and The Challenge of Inclusion: Gender Patterns in South And Central Asia* (2014), and *Exposing the Myths of Muslim Fertility* (2008). She has also published many research articles in national and international academic journals and edited books. Her areas of interest are gender and development, health and livelihood issues, minority issues including issues of Muslim women and their struggle for rights and entitlements both in the public and private domain, and identity issues. She has presented research papers in national and international seminars both within and outside the country. She has completed both minor and major research projects funded by various government agencies (University Grants Commission, New Delhi, Indian Council of Social Science Research, New Delhi and Ministry of Women and Child Development). She has been selected for the International Visiting Leadership Programme in the US and has been sponsored by UN-HABITAT and International Islamic University, Malaysia, to attend a workshop on land, property and housing rights in the Muslim world.

Suvendrini Perera completed her BA at the University of Sri Lanka and her PhD at Columbia University, New York. She is John Curtin Distinguished Emeritus Professor and Professor of Cultural Studies at Curtin University in Australia. She is author/editor of eight books, including *Australia and the Insular Imagination: Beaches, Borders, Boats and Bodies* (2009). A book based on the Deathscapes project, *Mapping Deathscapes: Digital*

Geographies of Racial and Border Violence, co-edited with Joseph Pugliese, was published with Routledge in 2021.

Ayman Qwaider is a researcher from Gaza, Palestine, now based in Australia with a Master's degree in Peace, Conflict and Development from the University of Jaume I (Spain). Throughout his career, he has participated in various research projects, latest of which was the Deathscapes Project (www. Deathscapes.org) and worked with several international organizations including UNESCO Paris and UNESCO Palestine. He is particularly interested in inclusive education and education in emergencies. Ayman has experience with community-based education projects in post-conflict contexts and working with people with disabilities. He is co-founder of Gaza Children Cinema, a community-based education initiative in Gaza that aims to provide a peaceful and a creative space where children can be children and where the overwhelming realities of siege, loss and war can be temporarily forgotten.

Mieka Smart is Assistant Professor at the College of Human Medicine (CHM) at Michigan State University, with appointments in the Division of Public Health and the Department of Epidemiology and Biostatistics. Currently, she evaluates global drug and alcohol policy, and investigates methods for overcoming barriers to clinical and public health research participation among marginalized populations, most especially in the context of COVID-19. She directs the Research to Reduce Disparities in Disease programme, a competitive NIH-funded research-training programme for medical students. She directs the CHM Leadership in Medicine for the Underserved (LMU) graduate certificate programme. Dr Smart teaches in the CHM Master of Public Health programme and the Master of Science in Global Health programme in the College of Osteopathic Medicine. Dr Smart earned her BA in public health, and MHS and DrPH in mental health from John Hopkins University. Contributors to Dr Smart's work for this volume include Megan Mulheron, Yvonee Nong, Crystal Juarez, Emiko Blalock, Roland J Thorpe Jr and Amanda Woodward.

Sunera Thobani is Professor in the Department of Asian Studies at the University of British Columbia. Her scholarship focuses on critical race, postcolonial and transnational feminist theory and politics; intersectionality and social movements; colonialism, Indigeneity and racial violence; globalization, citizenship and migration; Islam, Gender and Muslims in South Asian and Western media; South Asian Diaspora Studies; and South Asian Women's Gender and Sexuality Studies. Her publications include *Contesting Islam, Constructing Race and Sexuality: The Inordinate Desire of the West* (Bloomsbury Academic, 2020) and *Exalted Subjects: Studies in the Making of Race and Nation in Canada* (2007). She is also co-editor of *Asian Women: Interconnections* (2005) and *States of Race: Critical Race Feminist Theory for the 21st Century* (2010). Her research is published in numerous edited volumes and peer-reviewed journals, including *Borderlands*, *Atlantis*, *Feminist Theory*, *The Supreme Court Review*, *International Journal of Communication*, *Hypatia* and *Race & Class*. Dr Thobani has served as Ruth Wynn Woodward Endowed Chair in Women's Studies at Simon Fraser University and as the President of the National Action Committee on the Status of Women. She is a founding member of the cross-Canada network, Researchers and Academics of Colour for Equity (RACE). She is the recipient of the Sarah Shorten Award of the Canadian Association of University Teachers and a member of the Ethics Advisory Board for the Deathscapes project.

Xuezhi Du graduated from Huaibei Normal University with BA in Journalism in 2016 and graduated from Communication University of China with an MA in Theory and History of Communication in 2019. He is pursuing his doctoral degree in the School of Communication at Simon Fraser

University since 2020. His research mainly focuses on global communication, political economy of communication and rural communication. He is combining these three areas through his research on China's media policy and media transformation and its interaction with the world (especially with the Global South) under the context of (anti-)globalization. He has published several papers in leading Chinese communication journals including *China Publishing*, *Television Research* and *External Communication*.

Yuezhi Zhao is Humanities Chair Professor Tsinghua University, China and Professor Emiratus, Simon Fraser University, Canada. Dr Zhao has written extensively on the political economic and socio-cultural dimensions of China's rapidly transforming communication industries and the role of communication and culture in China's global integration. Her publications include *Sustaining Democracy? Journalism and the Politics of Objectivity* (1998), *Media, Market and Democracy in China* (1998), *Democratizing Global Media: One World, Many Struggles* (co-edited, 2005), *Global Communications: Toward a Transcultural Political Economy* (co-edited, 2008), *Communication in China: Political Economy, Power and Conflict* (2008), *Communication and Society: Political Economy and Cultural Analysis* (2011, in Chinese) and *Communication and Global Discursive Power Shifts* (co-edited, 2019, in Chinese).

ONE

Introduction

Sunera Thobani

Governments of all political stripes failed their populations in the COVID-19 pandemic.

The sacrifice of public health for political gain determined state responses, from liberal democracies to authoritarian regimes. In the US and UK, the failures were spectacularly evident in callous disregard; in Canada, they were cloaked in the language of compassion. The cruelty of the Western state was egged on by 'freedom movements' that flaunted going mask-less and vaccine-less as a fundamental right, even as racially exploited peoples across Africa, Asia, South/Central America – and in the West – pleaded desperately for ventilators, oxygen, vaccines, in short, for ' the universal right to breathe' (Mbembe, 2020).

The devastation wreaked by the pandemic was immediate. In the already underdeveloped Global South, skyrocketing rates of infection, death and deprivation obliterated decades of post-independence growth in a matter of months. In the West, white racist hatreds escalated in renewed vengeance against Black, Asian, Indigenous, Muslim and other minoritized communities. The global economy went into an astonishing tailspin that finally exploded the neoliberal myth of surging prosperity and endless growth.

True, the speed and force with which COVID-19 spread around the world caught governments by surprise. True also that public health officials initially assumed that the risk of contagion would be evenly distributed. Yet the social determinants of health that put racially minoritized communities and third world peoples at heightened risk of illness and death were not unknown when the pandemic hit. Nor did COVID-19 appear out of nowhere. This catastrophe was foreseeable. And, very likely, preventable. The fact that it was not brings into sharp relief the depths of the ethical-political morass in which the international order is mired.

The pandemic's first wave demonstrated that the risk of infection and death were gruesomely uneven along the North/South divide, and along their internal hierarchies of race, class, age, gender, citizenship, disability, religion, caste and sexuality. Yet the most powerful states responded with increased support for the corporate and business sectors, especially the big pharmaceuticals. As states poured massive subsidies into corporate hands, and protected their patent rights and profitability, immense wealth was generated for a small elite who made a killing from the virus (Collins, 2021). At the other end of the spectrum, the health of third world populations, and of frontline workers, mainly from racialized minorities, was of marginal concern in pandemic measures. The emergent COVID-19 economy profits off disease, fear and death, even as health care workers – worked to exhaustion – daily face illness and death. Yet despite the blow dealt them by the pandemic, racially exploited communities in the West and across the South are not entirely powerless. Their struggles for survival and livelihoods – in the face of intense violence and disenfranchisement – also came into sharper focus.

This book studies what COVID-19 reveals about the political, economic and cultural politics that organize contemporary national and global societies. Shattering triumphalist narratives of scientific invincibility and technical prowess that hold sway over the Western imaginary, COVID-19 exposed the ruthless political economic calculus of Western states and global elites. How did it all come to this? To ultra-right movements fighting public health measures that threaten their own, as well as the world's, survival? To round-the-clock funeral pyres, to corpses making their final silent pilgrimage along the most sacred of rivers in India? To the subjection of African countries to vaccine apartheid? Making sense of these deadly politics is the objective of this volume, centring the experiences of the dispossessed informs our research focus.

The chapters in this book take a historical approach to the conditions that gave rise to COVID-19. They show how states capitalized on the racial-class exploitations of earlier decades of privatization, austerity and imperialist wars during the pandemic to further extend the power of political and corporate elites over national and global institutions. It is this elite's grip on the means of communication that allowed it to regulate access to the information that shaped the pandemic's unfolding.

The tragic consequences of the Western derailment of an internationally coordinated pandemic response showed how stark remains the North/South divide. Undermining the World Health Organization's (WHO) attempt at such coordination, Western nation states instead fuelled anti-Asian racisms that allowed the virus to interact freely with the racial-colonial hierarchies that shape the global order. The ensuing health catastrophe has reinvigorated the relations of violence that reproduce these hierarchies. Previously existing gross disparities in income, healthcare, education, food security shaped access to COVID-19 testing and vaccines, to ventilators and personal protective equipment. Where neoliberalism had created jobless recoveries, the pandemic took care of the disposal of dispossessed sectors of populations. This book goes beyond the concerns of the moment to ask questions about the kind of world that is emerging from the pandemic as it reworks national and global hierarchies in cataclysmic ways.

Our study is grounded in a vision of global justice that approaches the pandemic as not only laying bare the fault lines of a social order based on profiting from the destruction of human and all life forms. The pandemic, we argue, underscores the urgent necessity for a way out of this death-oriented ethos. Highlighting the origin of the pandemic in environmental destruction (Cheema, 2020), we advocate for public health measures to confront global inequities and nurture the relatedness of all life forms. There is no other pathway to sustainable futures.

With politicians and public health officials failing the populations it is their responsibility to protect, families and friends, communities and even strangers, pulled together to provide care and sustenance, acting collectively to survive this catastrophe. It is in these relations of care, forged in socio-ethical bonds that crystallize collective responsibility and accountability, that we identify roadmaps to life-enhancing futures. Trusted community leaders and transparent organizations disseminated life-saving information and developed vital supports while political leaders continue privileging their economistic calculus, spreading disinformation, fostering nativism and promoting hate-filled propaganda.

Critiques of the profit-driven global economy are nothing new; repugnance at the ethical bankruptcy of corporate elites comes from many quarters. The need of the moment is for collective action to transform this socio-political order. As devastating as COVID-19 has been, it has also demonstrated that collective survival depends on justice, on humanizing social-economic relations, on protecting all life forms.

Making a global catastrophe

COVID-19, a zoonotic virus, jumped from an animal species to humans (Horton, 2020). This health problem quickly transmogrified into a racial-political crisis of epic proportion. COVID-19 may well go down in history as the turning point for the planet, given how closely it is imbricated with the imperialist-environmental crisis.

Given the ideologically charged, not to mention xenophobic, disinformation campaigns in our research sites, it is worth revisiting the conditions of emergence of COVID-19. It is popular knowledge that the virus was first identified in an outbreak in China, in December 2019. What is less known is that the history of this coronavirus is of longer duration, with multiple points of origin. Common in several animal and bird species, the virus had hundreds of variants before its transmission to humans. Six known variants have infected humans, the first in the Netherlands (2004), followed by Hong Kong (2005); COVID-19 is the seventh (Horton, 2020).

The first COVID-19 case was confirmed in Wuhan (30 December 2019), and local authorities issued a health alert the next day. The suspected site of transmission, an animal market, was immediately shut down and the WHO was notified. Upon confirmation of new cases (3 January), the WHO alerted the world (4 January), sent notification of a pandemic (5 January), and issued guidelines (10 January). Chinese scientists sequenced the genome of the virus and publicly shared this (12 January). Ominous news came the next day: COVID-19 had spread to Thailand. The WHO declared a Public Health Emergency (30 January) and called for an international response given the risk escalation (Horton, 2020). While the risk certainly proved severe, the world still awaits that globally coordinated response.

Western leaders quickly accused the Chinese state of deliberately spreading the virus.[1] Led by the US, the charge heightened the Western economic and political rivalry with China; it also distracted public attention away from Western states' failure to respond effectively to the growing public health threat.

In the years preceding the COVID-19 outbreak, critical scientists, Indigenous leaders, environmentalists and public intellectuals warned of the devastation being wrought on the environment, on local communities and animal species, by agri-business, urbanization, extractive industries, consumerist lifestyles and rampant tourism. The destruction of fragile ecosystems through land overuse, pollution and wars was often beyond repair, these conditions were catapulting the planet to a point of no return (Davis, 2005; Shiva, 1997). Many public health experts warned of the near-certainty of zoonotic diseases as wildlife habitats were shrinking drastically (Yong, 2020). As Mayer and Lewis note, 'the global health community has been acutely aware of and warning about the inevitable emergence of new pathogens that would constitute major threats to public health' for at least three decades (2020:1). It was therefore not surprising that ecofeminists immediately linked the new virus to the climate crisis, arguing 'It's the same cause' (Cheema, 2020).

Despite the warnings, governments continued pushing policies that worsened these conditions. States were restructured along with capital and labour through austerity and structural adjustment programmes. Publicly funded health care systems struggled as private healthcare flourished. More myopically, organizations specializing in disease control were put on the chopping block.[2] This restructuring was facilitated by the scapegoating of immigrants, refugees and migrants, constructed as 'scamming' scarce public resources. The resulting racial antagonisms shifted mainstream politics rightwards. Furthermore, two decades of US-led defeats in the war on terror fed the rise of ultra-nationalist movements; Islamophobia; racial violence; and deployment of lies in the service of militarization and securitization. These were the socio-political and cultural context for the incubation of the virus.

As the first COVID-19 cases began to mount, the anti-Chinese rhetoric deployed by the US president, the British prime minister and their allied leaders unleashed a wave of anti-Asian racism across the world. State (in)actions and public anxieties racialized the virus as 'Asian', a 'foreign invader'. A contagious disease spawned a racial crisis.

Despite the information coming from the Chinese scientific community, the WHO's declaration of the Health Emergency, and warnings from the University of Hong Kong about the dangers of travel and mass gatherings, it was mid-March before pandemic measures were introduced in Europe and

North America. Even then, the severity of the virus and the rapidity of its spread continued to be downplayed. In the US, the pandemic was dismissed as inconsequential ('a hoax') and the WHO was discredited ('covering up' for China). As thousands – soon millions – around the world became infected and started to die, the US withdrew support from the WHO. These attacks on the WHO would have terrible consequences for the world's population; the US withdrawal of its funds to the international agency amounted to a crime against humanity, argued the editor of *The Lancet* (Horton, 2020: 27). Thus was the fate of millions sealed.

The US administration's ridiculing of basic pandemic measures (masking, social distancing, quarantines) turned these into a new frontline for the culture wars. Rejecting masks and mocking vaccines became an assertion of white pride.

On the liberal front, governments that defended pandemic measures took to highlighting the 'newness' of the virus to explain their lack of preparedness and the chaotic way in which they implemented public health measures. The construction of a collective 'not-knowing' confined public awareness of COVID-19 to a narrow biomedical framework as the virus and its effects became delinked from the larger socioeconomic and political conditions of the societies in which the pandemic began to wreak havoc. Public confusion increased over subsequent waves of COVID-19 as the haphazard implementation of health measures left it to individuals to decide which to follow. When not engaged in direct disinformation, contradictory statements from politicians and health officials only added to the turmoil. In British Columbia, for example, pandemic measures were swiftly extended in the first lockdown, yet the Provincial Health Officer's daily exhortation to be 'compassionate' and 'kind' became the overriding message. These official slogans were visible and celebrated everywhere, yet workers of colour who provided care in hospitals and residential homes were left unprotected, without access to basic personal protective equipment.

As the pandemic ravaged particular communities, the state's willingness to sacrifice sectors of their population become evident. The ridiculing of pandemic measures in the US and UK were a strategy to develop herd immunity, the media reported. A top advisor to the Trump administration urged health officials to stand back: 'We want them infected', he apparently demanded, 'we essentially took off the battlefield the most potent weapon we had ... younger healthy people, children, teens, young people who we needed to fastly [sic] infect themselves, spread it around, develop immunity, and help stop the spread' (Diamond, 2020). While this impetus toward 'herd immunity' was tied to Trump's re-election bid, the UK government shared the approach.[3] Some health officials' warned that this strategy 'would unnecessarily put millions of people at risk of long-term complications and even death' (Diamond, 2020). This did not deter the Trump administration, which had worked hard to destroy 'Obamacare', a public healthcare plan to extend basic coverage to the US population. Not surprising, the US led the world in infection and death rates during the pandemic's first year (21, 045,468 cases and 357,166 deaths by 6 January 2021, *Hindustan Times*, 2021).

This sacrificial approach was operational also in our other research sites. The Indian prime minister, for example, announced a national lockdown for 1.3 billion people at four hours' notice (24 March 2020). The chaos that ensued set off a stunning reverse migration as millions of migrant workers – suddenly without access to food, employment or income support – began trekking back to their villages. Many would never make it, succumbing to thirst, hunger and exhaustion along the nation's highways. In the face of such desperation, 5,000 trains – *Shramik Specials* (Labourer Specials) – were organized to transport workers out of the cities. Jam-packed, these 'COVID trains' became super-spreaders as workers – the majority of them Dalit and Muslim – carried the virus with them (Gettleman et al, 2020). Healthcare services, already scarce in rural areas, were soon overwhelmed; thousands were also turned away at hospitals in the metropolitan centres. The International Labour Organization warned that 400 million informal sector workers were at risk of falling deeper into poverty (AFP, 2020).

This genocidal treatment of millions of dispossessed men, women and children was captured graphically in media reports. Chilling images of unprotected migrants being sprayed with disinfectants by health workers in full protective gear spoke volumes about the state's public health priorities (Ghani, 2020). India soon had the second highest reported infection rate (over 10 million cases and over 150,000 deaths in January 2021, *Hindustan Times*, 2021).[4]

In this catastrophic condition, Hindu nationalists escalated their attacks on Muslim minorities by dubbing them 'Corona Jihadis', redefining the pandemic as 'terrorism' (Frayer, 2020). The prime minister allowed the organization of mass political rallies, and the Kumbh Mela (a pilgrimage attracting millions of Hindu devotees), by declaring victory over COVID-19. Yet it was Muslims who were besieged by Hindu mobs who attacked them as a threat to the nation's health. Additionally, misinformation driven by 'fear, stigma, and blame' incited violence against the infected as well as the health care workers who cared for them (Menon et al, 2020).

Over in the UK, if ministers took no action to counter the viral spread in its first couple of months, British scientists, the cream of the crop, paid no heed to the warnings of Chinese scientists. The prime minister advised the public to 'take it on the chin' as infection rates rose; the government, '[f]or still unknown reason ... waited. And watched' (Horton, 2020: 50). Racism against Muslims had been a key factor in Brexit, yet it was Muslim doctors who were the first casualties of the pandemic within the National Health Service. Healthcare workers' pleas for protective gear went ignored, and it was not until mid-March (2020) that non-essential travel was clamped down on and the first schools went into lockdown. What initially appeared as the indecisive and unfocused actions of governments masked a decision to leave the virus well alone. As Johnson was later reported to have said, 'No more fucking lockdowns – let the bodies pile up' (Elgot and Booth, 2021).

Was this callous strategy based on early data which showed that Black and racial minorities, low wage and informal sector workers, the elderly and the already sick were being infected and dying in disproportionately high numbers? That rates of infection and the risk of death were much lower for the white middle and upper classes? Did these considerations shape the states' calculus of disposability? Was the seeming official incompetence reported daily an expression of the sacrificial logic of the state?

In the UK, mortality rates in the most deprived neighbourhoods were documented to be more than twice those in affluent areas, and people in the lowest income bracket were twice as likely to die as those in higher paid occupations (indie_Sage, 2020). In the US, it was the elderly, Black, Asian, LatinX and other communities of colour that were devastated by COVID-19, and then again by its economic fallout. To what extent did such data drive these governments' obfuscation of the science pointing to the pandemic's increasingly deadly hold? The answers to these questions became clearer in the shifts in the political landscape that followed as ultra-nationalist forces became more powerfully organized internationally – against public health measures – to contest the liberal-democratic order.

The association between race, age, class and infection and death rates was confirmed early in the pandemic, as was the susceptibility of those with pre-existing conditions (such as heart disease, diabetes and hyper-tension). Race, ethnicity and class were already well established as key social determinants of health before the pandemic (Gee and Ford, 2011). That COVID-19 would hit hardest those communities living in poverty, overcrowded and unsafe multigenerational households, and those who lacked access to housing, adequate income, food security and safe drinking water was entirely predictable. That an infectious disease would rampage quickly through slums and prisons, reservations and detention centres, refugee camps and migrants' quarters was also a certainty. These exacerbating conditions would hardly become ineffectual during any health crisis, even one sparked by a 'new' virus.

Pandemic measures were clearly designed from the perspective, experience and interests of the Western middle class family, from the vantage point of a nuclear family lifestyle and a professional worklife that could be readily switched online. Crimes against humanity? Trump's defunding of the WHO was only a drop in this grisly bucket.

Race, coloniality and the North/South divide

There is no clearer demonstration of the pandemic's remaking of the colour line – within and between societies in the Global North and South – than the issue of vaccines.

If the early warnings forecasting the looming catastrophe were previously unheeded by governments, so too were the warnings issued by some of their own public health officials in the pandemic's first wave about even deadlier waves to follow. Measures implemented during the first wave proved so ineffectual that public health officials in North America, the UK and much of Europe were soon overwhelmed by the extent of the subsequent infections and deaths they had *themselves* predicted.

The development of the vaccine was taken by many governments as the solution to COVID-19. Vaccines were subsidized, fast-tracked and then swiftly distributed in North America and Europe. Yet in the global context, socio-economic divisions were deepened in new ways as populations in Africa, the Middle East, South and Central Asia found virtually no access. The hoarding of vaccines by Western nation states prompted the WHO to plead against 'vaccine apartheid' (Shields and Farge, 2021). COVAX, the WHO's vaccine sharing programme on which the Global South depended, was itself heavily reliant on India's Serum Institute and donations from the West. Supply dried up as India became devastated by its own second wave. Even in these dire circumstances, the international patent regime prohibited states in the South from producing the life-saving medical breakthrough.

Protected by patents, vaccine production and distribution were harnessed to the drive for profits. Governments had subsidized pharmaceutical companies to develop the vaccine, provided them with vital government scientific expertise, and granted emergency approval to these vaccines. Big Pharma was then left free to charge governments for supply of these very same vaccines. Moderna, for example, received over US$1 billion from the US government, the company then charged the same government US$1.5 billion for 100 million vaccine doses (Stone, 2020). Calling for an immediate waiving of intellectual property rights over vaccines, African states demanded free sharing of knowledge and technology to ensure global access. These demands have been to no avail as the most powerful states continue to uphold the patent regime.

I have touched here on only a handful of pandemic measures; these are, however, remaking global and national relations of power. The chapters that follow discuss this remaking in eight sites: Australia, Bangladesh, Canada, China, India, Palestine, UK and the US. Providing snapshots of the pandemic, and studying the effects of key measures, we draw on interdisciplinary traditions (critical race theory, public health, gender and queer studies, international law, cultural and postcolonial studies) and activist frameworks (anti-racist, anti-capitalist, feminist, queer/trans and human rights) to demonstrate how COVID-19 is reshaping the forms of violence that shape these societies. We take an intersectional approach (Crenshaw, 1991) as we examine how race intersects with gender, class, caste, sexuality, nation and related social relations in shaping the pandemic itself, even as it restructures global society. Our piecing together of the treatment of Indigenous and other racialized communities in the North, and of dispossessed peoples in the underdeveloped South, reveals how race and coloniality are key vectors shaping the pandemic and its devastations.

Part I focuses on the racial–political economy and cultural politics of COVID-19. The chapters expand on the sacrificial logics, anti-Chinese racism, barriers to research participation and choice between life and livelihood presented to minoritized and migrant communities by various nation states. Part II addresses the deadly combination of settler occupation and de-development in Gaza, and of the underdevelopment and exploitation of women workers in South Asia. Part III highlights what lived experiences under lockdown reveal about the overlaying of earlier colonial-racial practices with the violence of the pandemic. These chapters highlight resilience, resistance and social care as vital to community making and collective survival.

Our studies show how states have yet to confront the conditions that led to this pandemic; consequently, public health (non)measures are dragging the world closer to the edge of an unfathomable precipice. The pandemic remains fast moving still, and our collection ends with a brief discussion of key conditions that require transformation for the prevention of further calamities. The fault lines we identify in the structure of the societies we study require urgent and radical change if the planet and its peoples are to escape being hurled over the abyss by the profit obsessed international order, with its death-dealing racial culture. The desire for a return to pre-pandemic 'normalcy' is now merged with the fascist politics of white supremacy. The following chapters emphasize how this 'normal' will plunge the planet and its peoples over the abyss. Dismantling the structures of violence that normalize such deadly calculations of the acceptable is the task put forward by COVID-19.

Notes

[1] The WHO scientific team corroborated Chinese scientists' accounts of COVID-19's emergence (Hernandez, 2021).

[2] The Trump Administration kept vacant its seat on the WHO Board and withdrew its scientist from China's Center for Disease Control (Yong, 2020).

[3] *The Guardian* (2020) reported that 'the concept [of herd immunity] was fundamental to the decision-making in the crucial months of February and March'. The government's own advisors publicly explained their plan was a 'controlled epidemic', 'a nice big epidemic', that would infect 60 per cent of the population (Horton, 2020: 51).

[4] The response of states was crucial in handling the lockdown's fallout. Thousands of shelters were set up in Kerala for returning migrants; for testing, contact tracing and community mobilization. This mitigated the viral spread and lowered mortality rates. In contrast, authorities in Maharashtra, with the highest case rates as at December 2020, used drones to track social distancing (Horton, 2020).

References

AFP (2020) 'Future is scary': Poor hit hardest by India coronavirus lockdown', Al Jazeera, 9 April. www.aljazeera.com/news/2020/4/9/future-is-scary-poor-hit-hardest-by-india-coronavirus-lockdown

Cheema, Z.S. (2020) 'It's the same cause': climate change and COVID-19 in the perspectives of environmental feminist activists', *Feminist Studies*, 46(3): 684–93.

Collins, C. (2021) 'Billionaire wealth, US job losses and pandemic profiteers', Inequality.org, 23 August. https://inequality.org/great-divide/updates-billionaire-pandemic/

Crenshaw, K. (1991) 'Mapping the margins: intersectionality, identity politics, and violence against women of colour', *Stanford Law Review*, 43(6): 1241–99.

Davis, M. (2005) *The Monster at Our Door*. The New Press.

Diamond, D. (2020) '"We want them infected": Trump appointee demanded "herd immunity" strategy, emails reveal', Politico, 16 December. www.politico.com/news/2020/12/16/trump-appointee-demanded-herd-immunity-strategy-446408

Elgot, J. and Booth, R. (2021) 'Pressure mounts on Johnson over alleged "let the bodies pile high" remarks', *The Guardian*, 26 April. www.theguardian.com/politics/2021/apr/26/pressure-mounts-on-boris-johnson-over-alleged-let-the-bodies-pile-high-remarks

Frayer, L. (2020) 'Hindu nationalists blame Muslims for India's COVID-19 crisis', NPR, 16 April. www.npr.org/2020/04/16/835710029/hindu-nationalists-blame-muslims-for-indias-covid-19-crisis

Gee, G. and Ford, C. (2011) 'Structural racism and health inequities: old issues, new directions', *Du Bois Review*, 8(11): 115–1332.

Gettleman, J., Raj, S., Yasir, S. and Singh, K.D. (2020) 'The virus trains: how lockdown chaos spread COVID-19 across India', *The New York Times*, 15 December. www.nytimes.com/2020/12/15/world/asia/india-coronavirus-shramik-specials.html

Ghani, H. (2020) 'Indian migrants sprayed with disinfectant chemical', *Al Jazeera*, 6 April. www.aljazeera.com/program/newsfeed/2020/4/6/indian-migrant-workers-sprayed-with-disinfectant-chemical

Guardian (2020) 'The Guardian view on herd immunity: yes, it was "part of the plan"', *The Guardian*, 29 April. www.theguardian.com/commentisfree/2020/apr/29/the-guardian-view-on-herd-immunity-yes-it-was-part-of-the-plan

Hernandez, J.C. (2021) 'Report backs China's idea on how virus first spread', *New York Times*, 10 February. www.nheducatorresources.com/eds?query=%22VIRAL%20transmission%22&type=DE&pagenumber=1&ff[]=SubjectGeographic%3Achina&searchfield=SU&ff[]=Journal:new%20york%20times

Hindustan Times (2021) 'India crosses 150,000 Covid-19 deaths: here's where other worst-hit countries stand', *Hindustan Times*, 6 January. www.hindustantimes.com/world-news/india-crosses-150-000-covid-19-deaths-here-s-where-other-worst-hit-countries-stand/story-MJYIpa2hfKUETwV592w4AI.html

Horton, R. (2020) 'Editorial', *The Lancet*, 395, 25 April.

Independent SAGE (indie_SAGE) (2020) *The Independent SAGE Report #21: COVID-19 and Health Inequality*, 13 November. www.independentsage.org/covid-19-and-health-inequality/

Mayer, J.D. and Lewis, N.D. (2020) 'An inevitable pandemic: geographic insights into the COVID-19 global health emergency', *Eurasian Geography and Economics*: 1–19. DOI: 10.1080/15387216.2020.1786425

Mbembe, A. (2020) *The COVID-19 Catastrophe*. Cambridge, UK: Polity Press.

Menon, V., Padhy, S.K. and J.I. Pattnaik (2020) 'Stigma and aggression against health care workers in India amidst COVID-19 times: possible drivers and mitigation strategies', *Indian Journal of Psychological Medicine*, 42(4): 400–01.

Shields, M. and Farge, E. (2021) 'WHO chief urges COVID-19 vaccine makers to advance doses for COVAX', *Reuters*, 17 May. www.reuters.com/business/healthcare-pharmaceuticals/who-chief-calls-vaccine-makers-advance-doses-covax-2021-05-17/

Shiva, V. (1997) *Biopiracy: The Plunder of Nature and Knowledge*. Boston, MA: South End Books

Stone, J. (2020) 'The people's vaccine: Moderna's coronavirus vaccine was largely funded by taxpayer dollars', *Forbes*, 3 December. www.forbes.com/sites/judystone/2020/12/03/the-peoples-vaccine-modernas-coronavirus-vaccine-was-largely-funded-by-taxpayer-dollars/?sh=20b53ace6303

Yong, E. (2020) 'How the pandemic defeated America', *The Atlantic*. www.theatlantic.com/magazine/archive/2020/09/coronavirus-american-failure/614191/

PART I

The Racial-Political Economy of COVID-19

TWO

Sacrificial Logics: The Racial Politics of COVID-19

Sunera Thobani

Introduction

Pandemics – spread with or without conscious human intent – are not new to North America. Indeed, the histories of pandemics remain inter-twinned with the histories of colonization of the Americas. Many infectious diseases (influenza, small pox, measles, and so on) came with the Europeans and ravaged Indigenous peoples across the continent, including in what would eventually become Canada (Daschuk, 2013).

The racialization of pandemics is also not novel in North America. Infectious diseases were deliberately spread to decimate native populations, their construction as 'savage' races justified their mass extermination (Daschuk, 2013). The effects of these early genocidal pandemics were magnified by the destruction of Indigenous food sources, and by the colonial state's starvation policies and withholding of medical assistance. The relation between pandemics, race and coloniality thus runs deep in the formation of Canada. Euro-Canadians also historically associated enslaved Black people and early Asian migrants, many indentured, with disease, filth and contagion. The construction of these communities as the source of racial pollution legitimized the violence and exclusionary policies directed toward them. Put differently, if the relation between infectious diseases, health catastrophes and colonialism is direct, so too is the relation between those for whom pandemics were a source of profit and power, and those who paid with their health and their lives. In this regard, the COVID-19 pandemic proved no exception.

Not the COVID-19 alert from Chinese scientists in early January 2020, nor the subsequent declaration by World Health Organization (WHO) of a global pandemic prompted concerted public health responses in Canada. A travel advisory to China was issued upon identification of the first case in Canada (25 January), and Canadians were flown back from China and quarantined (Dunham and Ho, 2020). It would take another six weeks before pandemic measures were introduced inside the country. As schools prepared to close for the mid-March Spring Break, a period of high vacation travel for middle class families, public health officials finally began to take the virus seriously. Lockdowns, quarantines and mandatory masking were implemented on the assumption that the pandemic's risk was now 'domestic' in addition to 'foreign'.

However, it soon became apparent that the impact of COVID-19 was vastly disproportionate; high levels of transmission appeared among racially minoritized and elderly communities. Anecdotal accounts in the media, community reports, and official statistics demonstrated this disproportionality. Accounts also surfaced of attempts by mostly racial minority healthcare and frontline workers to secure protective equipment in their workplaces. But pandemic measures – national and provincial – did not explicitly address these mounting racial-class–gender dimensions of infection and death rates.

The imposition of lockdowns and the move to online work revealed that public health measures were implicitly centring the experiences and lifestyles of the white, professional, nuclear family, which was at considerably lower risk of infection. 'Home' became constructed as a sanctuary from the virus, 'work' as portable and non-life threatening. Yet as the pandemic worsened, so too did its toll on racialized minorities. The absence of anti-racist approaches in public health measures, I argue, reveals a sacrificial logic that is reorganizing Canadian racial politics through the pandemic. The state's protection of the white nuclear family and its securing of corporate and business interests function through its sacrifice of the health and lives of racialized minorities, who work and live on the nation's economic and social 'frontlines'.

Workers of colour, particularly immigrant women and migrant workers, were known to be concentrated in healthcare, and other essential services. As I demonstrate below, the state and nation capitalized on the uneven distribution of risk to these communities, who were left mostly to their own devices for protection. This willingness to expose Indigenous and people of colour communities to the virus is remaking the nation's racial politics for the post-pandemic world.

The racial sacrifice

The sacrifice of individual life in service of the nation has been a crucial factor in the production of this entity, as Anderson recognized in his study of the modern nation (1983). Defining the nation as an 'imagined community' bound by a sense of common history and collective future, he argued that nationalism aligns and subjugates the individual's interests with those of the bourgeois elite who construct the national interest. Forging a community based on shared ethnicity, language and culture, nationalism crystallizes the citizen's loyalty to the nation state in the former's willingness to fight and die for the latter (Balibar and Wallerstein, 1988). This consensual willingness is what sustains the power of the state over the nation/al.

Mbembe, however, argues that sovereignty lies in 'the power and capacity to dictate who may live and who must die' (2003: 11). Critiquing Foucault's theorization of biopower – the modern form that disciplines the life of the Subject itself – Mbembe points out that modernity is shaped by multiple forms of sovereignty which include the state's, and its subject's, right to kill. In the colony, that underside of modernity, sovereignty is constituted through race. This is a formation wherein 'biopower', 'state of exception' and 'state of siege' are inextricably bound. Here, the 'sovereign right to kill is not subject to any rule ...', such that the 'sovereign might kill at any time or in any manner' (Mbembe, 2003: 25). As a civilizing power, sovereignty - and its subjects - constitute the Native as an 'absolute enemy', inhuman in their 'savage' nature, and thus condemned to die. This 'necropolitics' defines modern-colonial sovereign power.

In the pandemic, one sees an inversion of the logic of sacrifice inherent to nation-making as conceived of by Anderson. Here, it is not the national citizen who volunteers to sacrifice themselves to contain the viral threat. Rather, the state undertakes to protect this subject from the death that threatens its nationals by fortifying the 'frontline' with the nation's Other, the racialized 'essential service' worker, who is rendered sacrificial.

Mbembe's delineation of the death-dealing entailed in the production of sovereignty shows how 'necropolitics' constructs the enemy as utterly incommensurable. Yet the frontline worker is not the figure of this enemy. Nor is she the 'homo sacer' theorized by Agamben, an ancient figure who could not be sacrificed but could be killed with impunity. The frontline worker, Outsider though she is, can be – indeed, must be – tolerated, for her service to the nation is indispensable on a number of fronts (including as multicultural alibi for the 'post-racial' nation). Yet this figure's Otherness also makes her inessential. She is the alien within, neither racial-national kin nor political-citizen equal. Thus straddling the status of essential (worker) and inessential (non-national), she remains vital to the nation's coherence and prosperity. Hence it is primarily an economic calculus that organizes her inclusion while a racial animus inscribes her expendability. No moral calculus need be brought into play in her treatment; the rational calculus renders unnecessary the concern whether she lives or dies. After all, the longstanding underdevelopment, environmental devastation and wars looming over the Global South ensure there are plenty more lining up to replace her. The limits of racial-liberal democracy – its forms of inclusion – are evident in her dispensability.

COVID-19 made death an ever-present reality in the everyday spaces of the nation's life. This threat comes not from some violent interaction with an enemy, it is carried in the very air that sustains life. Paradoxically, the virus demonstrates how *this* threat of death, not in the abstract existential sense that animates Western philosophical treatises but in the corporeal-political sense, is racialized. If these treatises centre the subject citizen, they disappear the Native, the Immigrant and the Migrant, always-already sacrifice-able.

Centred on the citizen subject, pandemic measures have normalized the idea that it is politically and socially acceptable to risk the lives of those providing care, securing food supplies and maintaining the infrastructure, so that they continue to service the nation's health, welfare and economic survival. The sacrifice of these workers, their families and communities, is a utilitarian matter for the nation state.

How quickly this sacrificial logic was explicitly understood and embraced became visible in public expressions of appreciation for frontline workers who were being exposed to the risk of death as the condition of earning their livelihood. The mainly urban, white middle classes who took to 'celebrating' frontline workers every evening – banging pots and pans from the safety of their own porches and balconies, displaying 'thank you' signs in their windows and front yards – extolled the virtue of these workers. Such ritualistic outpouring of gratitude demonstrated how this 'thankfulness' functions in the economy of sacrifice to cement the pandemic's racial politics.

Foreign virus, alien threats

COVID-19 became fixed in the Canadian imaginary as a 'foreign' threat, given its early public linking with China, animal markets and Asian dietary practices. The assumption that COVID-19 was an 'Asian/Chinese' problem that would remain in 'China/Asia' racialized the virus, which helps explain the complacency among Canadian public health authorities even as infections were spreading across the country. This racialization of the virus drew public attention away from the conditions of its emergence, shaped by decades of neoliberal globalization, consumer capitalism and environmental degradation. COVID-19 became further racialized as Canadians began to avoid contact with Chinese/Asian Canadians. Chinatowns and Chinese-Canadian owned businesses, restaurants in particular, became the pandemic's early economic casualties. Asian-Canadians, particularly women, soon became targets for the racist attacks that would increase steadily through the pandemic's first year (by 700 per cent in Vancouver, BC for example, Zussman, 2021).

Other factors, no less ominous and just as enmeshed in racial geopolitics, had been reshaping Canadian political culture in the decades preceding the pandemic. The restructuring of social programmes escalated in the 1990s as spending cuts eroded health, education and social services (Thobani, 2007). Immigrant communities – code for racialized minorities – were scapegoated for overburdening social services. The liberal government of the time linked the restructuring to the immigration programme; the right-wing conservative government that followed further inflamed racial antagonisms as it implemented more cuts, including to Canada's Public Health Agency. Mandated precisely with tracking emerging health threats after the SARS outbreak (2003), the Public Health Agency was '... stripped of much of its capacity to gather outbreak intelligence and provide advance warning by the time the pandemic hit' (Robertson, 2020).

Hence even as neoliberal restructuring eroded the country's capacity to respond to public health threats, people of colour were constructed as a drain on the nation's resources. Such racialization would be compounded by Islamophobic discourse with the advent of the war on terror.

Moreover, specific weaknesses in the public health sector had been officially documented before the pandemic hit. An independent SARS commission was appointed in Ontario, the country's largest province, to investigate failures in dealing with that outbreak. This Commission identified 'a confluence of systemic weaknesses in worker safety, infection control and public health' in its first interim report; 'serious shortcomings in health protection and emergency management laws' in its second; and 'unresolved problems ... in health worker safety' in its final report (Campbell, 2006: 18–19). Pointedly noting that the country's largest province had no pandemic plan, the report concluded that 'The public health system was broken, neglected, inadequate and dysfunctional. It was unprepared, fragmented and uncoordinated. It lacked adequate resources, was professionally impoverished and was generally incapable of fulfilling its mandate' (Campbell, 2006: 17). The stage was thus set for the crisis that would soon erupt; public health agencies responded to COVID-19 as if the lessons of the earlier SARS epidemic had been expunged from memory.[1]

When the first COVID-19 lockdowns and quarantines began in mid-March 2020, the severity of the public health threat was not fully comprehensible, nor was it clear how extensively the pandemic would transform daily life. Variations in provincial health measures and the haphazard imposition of lockdowns, mask mandates and social distancing added to the sense of confusion. Public officials took to emphasizing the 'newness' of the pandemic to explain their earlier inaction, and the contradictory advice they now provided. Meanwhile, the pandemic was interacting with underlying structures of socioeconomic inequality: race, Indigeneity, age, class, gender, disability, among other factors. Early indications began to emerge of the unequal toll of the virus on Indigenous peoples and communities of colour, yet health officials took a 'race-neutral' approach to pandemic measures. The lack of response to the mounting (racial) evidence on the ground – in plain sight – reveals, I argue, a willingness to sacrifice the communities being devastated by the pandemic.

Settler ideology and COVID-19

Early in the pandemic, it became evident that Indigenous communities' health was expendable, despite the official embrace of 'reconciliation' and 'decoloniality' that was reshaping national politics on the recommendations of the Truth and Reconciliation Commission on the Residential School System (2015). I have already mentioned above the relation between pandemics and colonization that extended the mobility rights and territorial control of settler communities. Many Canadians resorted to this geographical-racial entitlement with the first COVID-19 lockdown. A white couple from Quebec travelled to a remote Northern First Nations community to shelter from the virus. Selling their belongings, they travelled across the country to their destination. They made no prior arrangements for accommodation, nor were they prepared for the cold (−30°C, noted Chief Dana Tizya-Tramm. He informed the couple they could not stay, given his own community of 250 members did not have adequate housing. As the Chief explained, 'they are actually putting themselves and our community in danger because we do not have a doctor in the community and one-fifth of our community are elders with most having underlying issues' (Miessner, 2020). The lack of access of many Indigenous communities to safe drinking water, housing and healthcare has been a matter of public record for many decades.

Yet upper middle class city dwellers headed to second homes and holiday resorts, many of these on, or close to, Indigenous reserves. Indigenous leaders responded by setting up checkpoints to protect their communities from the perils of such cross-border traffic. These attempts were met with public hostility. Settler colonialism, as Leonard argues, is enacted also 'through the entitled escapism of individuals, their movement, and occupation of multiple sites of residence for leisure evading Indigenous sovereignty and territoriality' (2020: 164). The national's right to leisure travel was upheld by provincial governments, who issued advisories but allowed resorts, spas, RV parks, and so on, to continue their operations as infections were mounting (Sterritt, 2020). Travel from pandemic-infected cities caused several viral outbreaks, as at the Whistler ski resort, endangering the health of Indigenous and other local communities.

Indigenous peoples, explain Starblanket and Hunt, 'are particularly vulnerable to communicable diseases due to longstanding and ongoing structural asymmetries that pertain to the administration of health services, environmental racism and the inaccessibility of healthy food sources' (2020: 5). Consequently, higher rates of chronic health conditions increased their susceptibility to COVID-19. Although provision of healthcare was included in the treaties signed by the colonial state, Canada 'has long refused to formally acknowledge that Indigenous people have Aboriginal or Treaty rights to health, remaining unclear about whether the provision of health services to Indigenous people follows from policy, statute, or treaty. This situates Crown treaty commitments as discretionary and contingent on social and political will', argue Starblanket and Hunt (2020: 9). The treatment of treaty rights as discretionary and conditional, along with their compartmentalization, allows the state to deny and/or fragment the claims of treaty nations. The bifurcation of Indigenous rights from their access to healthcare, as well as the obfuscation of both by various levels of government, remains central to the suppression of Indigenous title, argue Starblanket and Hunt (2020).

With its politically expedient approach to Indigenous title, the Trudeau government took pandemic conditions to defer obligations to Indigenous nations. At the height of the health crisis, the government announced it would not meet its target to ensure safe drinking water on reserves, many of which have lived with unsafe water for decades (Stefanovich, 2020a). The government also announced a delay in the release of its National Action Plan on Murdered and Missing Indigenous Women, with no revised timeline (Stefanovich, 2020b). Moreover, while the federal government is responsible for providing vaccines on reserves, more than half of the Indigenous population lives in densely populated urban centres, with high levels of poverty, addiction and unemployment (Anderson, 2019). Obfuscation regarding which level of government bears responsibility for these urban Indigenous communities left them without clearly identifiable access to COVID-19 vaccines (CBC Radio, 2021).

The deferral of Indigenous title and Aboriginal rights reveals the sacrificial logic that continues to shape the nation state's treatment of these communities. The treaty relationship was poisoned by the colonial politics that harnessed treaty making to the destruction of Indigenous life-worlds. This approach informed the liberal state's construction of the nation, its interests, in the pandemic.

Essential workers, inessential lives

Early media reports revealed the rapid spread of COVID-19 in residential care facilities; outbreaks were soon reported on farms and in meat packing plants. These sectors are heavily reliant on workers of colour – migrants and immigrants – who are paid low wages and work in precarious conditions. Overrepresented also in health, medical and personal care; retail, hospitality and service sectors; agriculture and transportation, workers of colour were now situated in the pandemic's frontlines. Immigrant women, for example, made up 31 per cent of nurse aides, orderlies and health service providers in 2016, these ratios were much higher in the major cities (78.7 per cent in Toronto, 71.7 per cent in Vancouver, 70.5 per cent in

Calgary and 62.4 per cent in Edmonton) (Turcotte and Savage, 2020). These metropolitan centres were where the pandemic raged. In Toronto, 83 per cent of all reported COVID-19 cases were among people of colour communities, as were 71 per cent of hospitalizations (Cheung, 2020). While poor housing conditions, high poverty rates, perilous work conditions, limited access to services and discrimination contributed to this gross disparity, the 'race-blind' approach of public measures compounded COVID-19's disproportionate effects.

These conditions became dire with the second wave. Twenty per cent of all COVID-19 cases were documented among healthcare workers, which was double the rate for these workers at the global level (Possamai, 2020). Moreover, healthcare workers reported 75 per cent of all COVID-19 related workplace injuries. Adequate protection was not provided to them; the demands of the unions who represent them were dismissed by health authorities. These workers also often received misleading information about workplace safety protocols. Such conditions prompted the president of the second largest Trade Union Confederation in Quebec to state, 'We have been abandoned. The term is strong, but it represents the reality. Public health recommendations, blindly followed by health institutions, have failed to protect staff. And health care workers continue to be put at risk' (Possamai, 2020: 10–11). These workers also bore the brunt of public anger over pandemic measures.

The economic reliance on the racialized labour of Black, Asian, Latinx and other communities has shaped Canadian immigration and citizenship policies for decades (Thobani, 2007). These policies have also contributed to the making of racial/ethnic enclaves within the country (Dua, 2007), including *de facto* racially differentiated neighbourhoods. The racial-spatial politics of urban space virtually ensured uneven distribution of the viral risk, which was soon evident in residential areas as well as workplaces.

Neighbourhoods with higher concentrations of communities of colour were more likely to have higher COVID-19 death rates in three of Canada's largest provinces, reported Statistics Canada (Carman, 2020). In British Columbia, mortality rates were ten times higher in communities with greater than 5 per cent ethnic minorities. The attitude of public health officials in this province to the collection of such race-based data is instructive. While the Provincial Health Minister was reported to support collecting such data, her office stated that 'due to the surge in cases and demand on public health resources, data on race is not currently being collected at the point of care, with the exception of data on Indigeneity' (Carman, 2020). This exception regarding Indigenous peoples was seen by Indigenous activists as an attempt to avoid political scandal over the treatment of Indigenous peoples. The unwillingness of health authorities to track the racialized spread of the pandemic, in the face of government reports pointing to the racialized distribution of risk, suggests more than benign neglect. One sees the political will to capitalize on the racialized structures of inequality, and on political marginalization, to tolerate, perhaps even intensify, the risk of infection and death among communities of colour.

Such capitalization of racialized risk is visible in publicly reported account after account of working conditions in residential care homes and hospitals (CFNU, 2020; Bailey, 2021); public transit and long distance trucking (Aguilar, 2020; Irvine, 2020); farms and meat packing plants (Migrant Workers' Alliance for Change, 2020); and prisons (House and Rashid, 2021). Not surprising, 21 per cent of Black people reported knowing somebody who died from COVID-19 in contrast to 8 per cent of non-Black Canadians; and neighbourhoods with diverse communities (over 10 per cent Black) reported four times higher COVID-19 hospitalization rates and twice the number of deaths (age-adjusted) than less diverse areas (less than 0.5 per cent Black) (DasGupta et al, 2020).

As infection rates increased during the second wave of COVID-19, South Asian communities were represented as deliberately increasing the risk of infections and endangering the nation in media reports. Extended family structures and multigenerational households were linked to the spread of the virus. South Asian religious and cultural practices were also identified as endangering these communities, hence particularly reprehensible. Community gatherings to celebrate Diwali, the new year, were depicted as irresponsible, even though of the more than 100 places of worship, only one was issued with a fine in this climate of heightened surveillance. In contrast, neither Thanksgiving nor Christmas gatherings were the subject of such sensationalized reporting. Meanwhile, the culturally appropriate pandemic practices developed in these communities – including special masks to accommodate turbans and public awareness campaigns in diverse languages – went ignored.

Seasonal workers, unseasonal hostility

'We need permanent resident status on landing, with open work permits. Contracts that limit us to one employer create fear and abuse. With permanent status and open permits, that fear will be much less. Not everyone wants to live here but we want the same rights as Canadians have', stated a letter from over 100 migrant workers to Employment and Social Development Canada and Immigration, Refugee and Citizenship Canada (Migrant Workers' Alliance for Change, 2020). The letter noted that these workers pay into the Employment Insurance Program yet are ineligible to claim unemployment benefits. It also noted that many do not have safe drinking water, and often live ten to a room in bunkhouses without heating, ventilation or air conditioning. The letter was sent in August 2018, 16 months before the pandemic, and no response was received from either of the two government Departments it addressed. Instead, pandemic measures enhanced the vulnerability of these workers, who constitute a vital component of the *Canadian* workforce, by enhancing their employers' powers to control them.

As the category 'essential worker' was transformed in the pandemic, a range of low wage, part time, seasonal and insecure workers came to public attention as vital to the nation's health and welfare. From harvesting vegetables to processing meat, the indispensability of the 'invisible' migrant worker came into sharp focus. Made indiscernible in the register of the 'worker', as well as in the labour movement's calculus of the *Canadian* worker, the role of migrant workers was now recognized as essential to the nation's survival of the pandemic.

But even as the pandemic drew public attention to these workers' indispensability, pandemic measures revealed the lengths to which the state and employers would go to deprive them of the most basic rights. If 'we' owe the frontline workers our lives, as Horton (2020) recognized, 'their' lives were put on the line for the low wages they receive in return.

The Canadian agri–business sector is controlled by big corporations that have been taking over small and mid-sized farms; this sector was worth C$111.9 billion of 2016 GDP, and C$62.6 billion in exports. Four corporations control meat production, five companies control 80 per cent of the retail grocery market, three plants process 85 per cent of the country's beef (Migrant Workers' Alliance for Change, 2020). As COVID-19 outbreaks were reported on farms and meat processing plants, the systems of control that regulate these workers' mobility were refortified, in effect heightening the risk to their lives.

With the first lockdown, Canadian borders were closed off to most non-citizens but remained open – with disruptions – for migrant workers. Once arrived, they were required to quarantine in their place of employment. Those headed to work on farms were housed in bunkhouses, which, at the best of times, were overcrowded and had inadequate facilities. These bunkhouses became vectors for the disease; outbreaks were reported at more than 30 farms in Ontario. In many cases, employers reportedly made their workers sign away any rights they might have in order to stay and work on the farms, a situation likened to 'being in prison' by migrants (CBC, 2020). Pandemic restrictions on their mobility intensified these workers' dependence on employers: they were now reliant on employers for any movement from their worksite for any purpose whatsoever.

Despite finding themselves in such perilous conditions, without residency or mobility rights, migrants organized to lobby the government for residency rights, open work permits, healthcare and unemployment benefits. These campaigns met little success. Exactly the opposite was the case for the businesses that rely on, and profit from, withholding these very rights (migrants made up over 40 per cent of agricultural workers in Ontario and over 30 per cent in British Columbia, Quebec and Nova Scotia in 2017). These profits were buttressed as the agri-business sector received C$1 billion in state support; as the Migrant Workers' Alliance for Change's report explained, 'Canada invests public money into agri-business expansion, and not into ensuring decent working conditions or immigration rights for the workers who sustain it' (2020: 11). Migrant workers reported working up to 16 hours a day, with no social distancing measures, inadequate food and safe drinking water, and no overtime for working additional hours. The lack of regulation of their working and living conditions during the pandemic, like the denial of residency rights and access to social supports, demonstrates the willingness of the state and Canadian employers to sacrifice these workers to the pandemic.

Conclusion

Pandemic measures gave a new lethality to processes of racialization in Canada, a settler society that claims to be presently engaged in processes of 'decoloniality'. Yet the collective willingness to expose Indigenous peoples and racially minoritized communities to greater risk of infection and death during the pandemic in the ways described above points to a sacrificial logic which, I have argued, can be traced to the originary racial–colonial foundation of this nation state. Recourse by public health officials to the claim that the pandemic was 'new', and hence evaded control, obfuscated the actuality that its racialized consequences were not only predictable but unfolded in plain sight. It is this predictability that leads me to argue that capitalization of existing racial hierarchies became publicly acceptable as the means to national survival of the pandemic.

How far has this sacrificial logic become normalized? How will it play out in the catastrophes yet to come? Although Black, Asian, Indigenous and other communities of colour are ill-served by the Canadian state, the political economy of this nation state, its healthcare system and other essential services rely heavily on the labour of the nurses, doctors, support staff, technicians, migrants who come from these minoritized communities. The sacrificial logic brought to the fore by COVID-19 demonstrates the limits of 'inclusion' in this nation state's institutions.

Note

[1] See the SARS Commission website: www.archives.gov.on.ca/en/e_reco rds/sars/about/index.html

References

Aguilar, B. (2020) 'Eight TTC maintenance workers walk off job as union demands more COVID-19 testing', CTV News, 18 April. https://toronto.ctvnews.ca/eight-ttc-maintenance-workers-walk-off-job-as-union-demands-more-covid-19-testing-1.4902579

Anderson, B. (1983) *Imagined Communities: Reflections on the Origin and Spread of Nationalism.* Verso.

Anderson, T. (2019) 'Results from the 2016 census: housing, income and residential dissimilarity among Indigenous people in Canadian cities', *Statistics Canada*, 10 December.

Bailey, I. (2021) 'Nurses raise alarm over COVID-19 vaccine access, distribution issues across BC', *The Globe and Mail*, 6 January.

Balibar, E. and Wallerstein, I. (1998) *Race, Nation, Class: Ambiguous Identities*. Verso.

Campbell, The Honorable Mr. Justice Archie (2006) *'Thirteen Essential Questions', Spring of Fear: Executive Summary: Volume One*. SARS Commission (18–19), December.

Carman, T. (2020) 'COVID-19 mortality rate higher in neighbourhoods with more visible minorities', *CBC News*, 17 November. www.cbc.ca/news/canada/british-columbia/covid19-minorities-health-bc-canada-1.5801777

CBC (2020) 'Bitter Harvest: the story of the pandemic and the people who pick our food', *The Fifth Estate* (TV documentary), season 46, episode 2, first aired 30 November.

CBC Radio (2021) 'On the Coast', 1 February, hosted by Gloria Macarenko.

CFNU (2020) 'What happened to PPE production in Canada', joint statement by CFNU, OCHU and Green Jobs Oshawa, 25 September.

Cheung, J. (2020) 'Black people and other people of colour make up 83% of reported COVID-19 cases in Toronto', *CBC News*, 30 July. www.cbc.ca/news/canada/toronto/toronto-covid-19-data-1.5669091

Daschuk, J. (2013) *Clearing the Plains: Disease, Politics of Starvation and the Loss of Aboriginal Life*. University of Regina Press.

DasGupta, N., Shandal, V., Shadd, D., Segall, A. and in conjunction with CivicAction (2020) 'The pervasive reality of anti-black racism in Canada: The current state, and what to do about it', BCG, 14 December. www.bcg.com/en-ca/publications/2020/reality-of-anti-black-racism-in-canada

Dua, E. (2007) 'Exclusion as inclusion', *Gender, Place & Culture*, 14(4): 445–66.

Dunham, J. and Ho, S. (2020) 'Can I see her any sooner?' *CTV News*, 7 February. www.ctvnews.ca/canada/can-i-see-her-any-sooner-father-reunites-with-daughter-in-canadian-quarantine-zone-1.4801361

Horton, R. (2020) 'Editorial', *The Lancet*, Vol. 395, 25 April.

House, J. and Rashid, A. (2021) 'Failure to protect essential prisoner workers undermines public safety', *The Bullet*, 5 January. https://socialistproject.ca/2021/01/failure-to-protect-essential-prisoner-workers-undermines-public-safety/

Leonard, K. (2020) 'Medicine lines and COVID-19: Indigenous geographies of imagined bordering', *Dialogues in Human Geography*, 10(2): 164–8.

Miessner, D. (2020) 'Quebec couple who fled to remote Indigenous community to avoid COVID-19 sent back: Chief', *The Canadian Press*, 31 March. https://globalnews.ca/news/6758430/coronavirus-quebec-couple-indigenous-yukon/

Migrant Workers' Alliance for Change (2020) *Unheeded Warnings: Covid-19 and Migrant Workers in Canada*, 8 June. https://migrantworkersalliance.org/policy/unheededwarnings/

Possamai, M. (2020) A Time of Fear: How Canada failed our health care workers and mismanaged COVID-19. Consultant Report. https://www.atimeoffear.com/

Robertson, G. (2020) ' "We are not prepared": The flaws inside public health that hurt Canada's readiness for COVID-19', *The Globe and Mail*, 26 December.

Starblanket, G. and Hunt, D. (2020) *COVID-19, The Numbered Treaties & The Politics of Life*. A Special Report. The Yellowhead Institute. June.

Stefanovich, O. (2020a) 'Indigenous Services minister acknowledges Liberals won't meet promised drinking water target', *CBC News*, 2 December. www.cbc.ca/news/politics/indigenous-services-minister-drinking-water-target-1.5824614

Stefanovich, O. (2020b) 'Ottawa delays release of national action plan', *CBC News*, 26 May www.cbc.ca/news/politics/stefanovich-mmiwg-action-plan-delay-1.5583585

Sterritt, A. (2020) 'Indigenous Leaders say they should have been consulted before B.C. government eased pandemic measures', *CBC News*, 26 June. www.cbc.ca/news/canada/british-columbia/indigenous-people-say-not-consulted-before-reopening-of-bc-1.5627464

Thobani, S. (2007) *Exalted Subjects: Studies in the Making of Race and Nation in Canada.* University of Toronto Press.

Turcotte, M. and Savage, K. (2020) 'The contribution of immigrants and population groups designated as visible minorities to nurse aide, orderly and patient service associate occupations', StatCan COVID-19: Data to Insights for a Better Canada, *Statistics Canada*, 22 June.

Zussman, R. (2011) 'Horgan "deeply troubled" by 717% increased in anti-Asian hate-crimes in Vancouver', *Global News. February* 17. https://globalnews.ca/news/7647135/horgan-bc-presser-feb-18/

THREE

Racism, Anti-Communism and COVID-19: The Making of a Transnational Discursive War Against China

Yuezhi Zhao with Xuezhi Du

China was the first country to report cases of the coronavirus, SARS-CoV-2, in late December 2019. This fateful fact coupled with a racist and anti-communist 'new Cold War' discursive structure produced some of the most hateful media discourses against China in the early stage of the pandemic. Furthermore, just as US-dominated racial capitalism is transnational, this discursive structure is also transnational in nature, with important resonance within China itself.

We first identify some of the intertwining discursive features of the US-led Western media's COVID-19 coverage that are racist and anti-communist in nature. We then focus on the 'Fang Fang Diary' case to reveal the making of a transnational discursive alliance. In arguing that it is not just racism, but the intersection of racism and anti-communism that is at the core, we argue that whether China as it is today is a 'truly' communist country is not the concern here. As far as the Western dominant discourse is concerned, so long as China is ruled by the Communist Party of China (CPC), it is its antithesis. Moreover, we are not evaluating China's success or failure in dealing with COVID-19, nor are we addressing how different social-economic groups in China have fared under COVID-19.

The context

When China locked down the city of Wuhan to contain the COVID-19 outbreak in late January 2020, the country was already dragged into full-blown trade and technological wars with the US. The 2008 global financial crisis had made the existing form of US–China economic integration unsustainable (Zhao, 2014). Furthermore, with a Xi Jinping leadership expressing a commitment to uphold China's existing political system in 2012, the ruling US elite realized that they had once again 'lost' China, in a way that is analogous to their 'loss' of China to the international communist movement in 1949.

This is a ruling US consensus that transcends racial and gender divides. The 'pivot to Asia' strategy, which aimed at containing China in the post-2008 era, was launched by the Obama administration. Perhaps more tellingly, it was Kiron Skinner, a female African American foreign policy maker who, in her capacity as the then Director of Policy Planning at the US Department of State in the Trump administration, pointed out in April 2019 that by comparing interactions with China with the Cold War with the USSR, which is a 'fight within the Western family', the US is engaging in a fight with 'a great power competitor that is not Caucasian' (Zheng, 2019). Although Skinner was singled out for intra-elite rebuttals for her overt racist remarks (cf. Ward, 2019), this did not conceal the fact that, well before the outbreak of COVID-19, a new Cold War against China was already in the making, setting the stage for the weaponization of COVID-19 against China. In fact, if the domestic US dimension of racial capitalism has meant the systematic marginalization and discrimination of Black people and other peoples of colour, the global dimension of racial capitalism has meant the systematic demonization and even subversion of states that dare to take a different political form and, more crucially, dare to struggle for some sense of justice and equality in the global arena.

'The real sick man of Asia'

The *Wall Street Journal* (WSJ) led a racist discourse by publishing conservative foreign policy scholar Walter Russell Mead's article, 'China is the real sick man of Asia', on 3 February 2020. 'The sick man of Asia' was a well-known insult against the Chinese in the aftermath of the Opium War, symbolizing not only China's subjugation to Western colonial powers, but also the literal sickness of the Chinese to opium addiction. That such an old colonial trope would be used in a headline in the 21st century during the early stage of the COVID-19 outbreak underscores the deeply ingrained nature of racism. Subsequent revelations and fallouts reinforce the point that this is not incidental, but a calculated provocation by the WSJ's top management (Tracy, 2020). Furthermore, the Chinese government's demand for an apology was seen as unjustified. In this view, the CPC-led Chinese state has no legitimacy in securing the dignity of the Chinese nation in the international discursive realm.

'China's Chernobyl'

Not only does the Chinese state have no legitimacy in defending Chinese national dignity, it is a state that should have collapsed long ago – or at least this has long been the wish. The outbreak of COVID-19 provided an irresistible opportunity for the 'China collapse' discourse to rear its head. Given that the Chernobyl nuclear power plant incident was widely seen as a pivotal disaster that led to the collapse of the USSR, the invocation of 'China's Chernobyl' analogy in the initial coverage of COVID-19 reveals the deeply anti-communist nature of the Western media. A Nexis-Lexis search for the keywords 'China', 'Chernobyl' and 'coronavirus' from 1 December 2019 to 25 December 2020 yielded as many as 5,172 items. Among the ten leading titles that published the most items with a combination of these three keywords are the *New York Times*, *The Times*, *The Guardian*, *The Sun*, *The Independent*, and *The Mirror*. The *Washington Post*'s 11 February 2020 article entitled 'China's Chernobyl? The coronavirus outbreak leads to a loaded metaphor' plays a tone-setting role. Referring to the Chernobyl incident as 'a preamble to the collapse of the Soviet Union' and illustrative of the US media elite's shared perspective on this, the article cites Tom Rogan of the *Washington Examiner* as saying that Chernobyl and the coronavirus have clearly 'shared truths', that is, '[t]hese are two terrible accidents, dramatically worsened by grotesque mismanagement and magnified by avoidable secondary injustices at the highest levels of the state' (Tharoor, 2020).

The WSJ elevated the Chernobyl metaphor to its anti-communist ideological high note with an article by somebody who experienced Chernobyl. On 13 February 2020, two days after the *Washington Post* article, the WSJ published an article by Yavoslav Trofimov entitled 'From Chernobyl to the coronavirus', with a subtitle that makes a seamless connection between the old Cold War against the USSR and the new Cold War against China: 'In the USSR in 1986, as in China today, a public health disaster exposed the limits of dictatorial rule' (Trofimov, 2020). True to trite anti-communist tropes, suppression of information and denial of bad news are standard story ingredients. Thus, even though China's experience in dealing with SARS in 2003 turned out to be relevant in the country's public health system's identification of the new virus in 2019, the historical relevance of SARS was only limited to the authorities' initial suppression of information. After all, as far as the discourse of anti-communism is concerned, nothing is new under the sun, and China, so long as it remains under the CPC's dictatorial rule, will not be able to learn a thing from the SARS experience. Furthermore, even though it was Dr Zhang Jixian, a female doctor who first treated patients with this new virus and was vigilant enough to report the situation through official channels between 26–29 December 2019, it was Dr Li Wenliang, with his unauthorized social media posting of an internal medical report about the unknown virus among his classmate circles, who earned the status of a 'whistleblower' and became an instant Western media celebrity. The anti-communist discourse needs a 'whistleblower' and a freedom fighter, and even better, a martyr. Dr Li, with his mistreatment by public security officials for his unauthorized information release and then with his unfortunate death after contracting COVID-19, fitted such a role.

Leading US politicians are also at the forefront to promote the Chernobyl metaphor. 'Coronavirus "cover-up" is China's Chernobyl – White House Adviser' – the title of this 24 May 2020 Reuters dispatch is highly illustrative of the extent to which US government officials and media outlets mutually reinforced each other to propagate a racist and anti-communist symbolic environment against China (Chiacu, 2020). In the same way that the US press played a pivotal role in amplifying Senator Joseph McCarthy's anti-communist accusations in the 1950s, mainstream US media, despite its apparent adversarial position against the Trump administration, faithfully reported accusations against China by US politicians as news. Furthermore, the US media themselves provided the stage for high-level government officials to deploy their 'weapons of mass distraction' by making China into a scapegoat. The logic of sensationalism, in the context of growing competition from online news sources and social media outlets, has meant that the more inflammatory, the better.

In Canada, Conservative leadership candidate Peter Mackay also joined an anti-China Western political alliance to chant the 'China's Chernobyl moment' mantra. Instead of preparing themselves to fight against a pandemic at the home front, some foreign politicians used COVID-19 to wage their ideological war against China by issuing a call for 'people around the world to confront "an inconvenient truth" about China' (Connolly, 2020). The CCP-led Chinese state, built in opposition to the imperialist powers, was thus recast in US political discourse as a threat to the world's people.

'China virus' and 'Wuhan virus'

It took Donald Trump, who had by early 2020 mobilized the US state to wage all-out trade and technological wars against China (Lim, 2019), to weaponize COVID-19 in an escalation of the epic struggle between US and China. By late March 2020, the US had lost a crucial window of opportunity to prepare for a fight against COVID-19 in its own heartland. It was within this context that we must understand Trump's uses of the 'China virus' label in reference to COVID-19, long after the World Health Organization adopted COVID-19 as a standard medical name for the coronavirus.

Trump initially did not use the 'China virus' label in his social media messages. He first used the term on Twitter on 16 March 2020. There was strong evidence that Trump did not only decide to use the 'China virus' label deliberately, but he also did so opportunistically. We can outline several reasons. First, in the initial stage of the struggle against the disease, China was the epicentre. As such, Trump could express a patronizing attitude toward an embattled China. Even though his administration was warned as early as January 2020 about the likelihood of COVID-19 becoming a pandemic, he refused to take proactive measures to prepare for an imminent battle against the virus for fear of a stock market meltdown. Later, as the Trump administration found itself ill-prepared for the outbreak in the US, the political survival instinct to find a scapegoat became much stronger. Instead of leading the US to fight a well-prepared war against COVID-19, Trump opted to use racist labels for the disease to divert US domestic public anger away from his administration.

Second, because the exact origin of the virus has been a matter of controversy, Trump's use of the 'China virus' label could be seen as an offensive strategic attempt to put China on the defensive. As more pieces of information were revealed, with some speculating the possible origin of the virus in the US military, voices inside China's social media, and even within China's foreign ministry spokespeople circles, had demanded an explanation from the US side for the spreading of the virus. Within such a context, Trump's repeated use of the 'China virus' label could be interpreted as a combative US presidential deployment of a dangerous rhetorical weapon of destruction in his continuous war against China. In this sense, Trump had acted rationally and cool-mindedly. That is, there is 'rationality' in his apparent irrationality or craziness.

Finally, the fact that China had by mid-March 2020 achieved initial success in containing the virus through decisive measures, thus damping any wishful thinking on the part of some US elites on the prospects of the highly anticipated 'collapse of China', had perhaps further irritated Trump, making him even more aggressive and desperate to resort to racism to stigmatize and provoke China. Although Trump, in response to criticisms by Asian Americans in the US, subsequently stopped using the 'China virus' label and tweeted on 23 March 2020 that people should 'protect our Asian American community' and that 'the spreading of the Virus … is NOT their fault', this did not end the US government's smear campaign against China. US Secretary of State Mike Pompeo even attempted to use 'Wuhan virus' in a joint statement on COVID-19 at a G7 foreign ministers' meeting on 25 March 2020 (Finnegan, 2020).

'Dr Shi Zhengli made COVID-19' and 'China must pay'!

A society's symbolic spaces and actual physical spaces are closely related. Before long, hateful graffiti espousing conspiracy theories, personalized in the most telling tale of 'Dr Shi Zhengli made COVID-19,[1] had appeared on public spaces in North

America, making the entire symbolic environment highly hostile and threatening for Chinese Americans and the larger community of Asian Americans. Reports of COVID-19 related and racially motivated assaults on Asian Americans confirmed the real world consequences of such a hateful symbolic environment against China (Nair, 2020; Young, 2020).

With the assignment of responsibility comes demands for accountability. The next narrative plot in the racist and anti-communist discourse, then, is for China to pay for the virus. Here again, what must be emphasized is this: racism and anti-communism mutually reinforce each other, and real material interests and the terms of capitalist accumulation are being fought out in the global political economic and cultural struggles over COVID-19. If the 'China collapse' trope remains too general, then, there were more specific ways in which US elites and their racist and anti-communist allies in the rest of the world wish to profit from a discourse on 'China responsibility'. Analogous to how the colonial powers had once extracted the infamous 'Boxer (Gengzi) Indemnity' from China in the year 1900 in the aftermath of the Boxer War, China must be made to pay for the virus in 2020 – which also happened to be a 'Gengzi' year in the Chinese lunar calendar. On 16 March 2020, the same time that Trump used the 'China virus' label, US Congressman Jim Banks of Indiana made the shocking statement on Fox News that President Trump should refuse to honour the US debt that China holds as a form of compensation for the 'burden and cost' incurred by the US due to COVID-19. This ushered in a whole spade of extortions, lawsuits and other claims aiming to make China pay for COVID-19 related damage (Tyler, 2020; Quinn, 2020; Ritter, 2020; Tan, 2020; Fan, 2020).

The insidious and ridiculous nature of these lawsuits lies not just in their complete disregard for sovereign equality of the interstate system as established by the Westphalia framework and reaffirmed by the UN Charter (Fan, 2020). Rather, it lies in these anti-China crusaders' lack of understanding of the very nature of the CPC-led Chinese state. Stephen Dinan's following report of the Missouri case underscores the profoundly comical nature of the case: 'Even if sovereign immunity isn't waived for China itself, Mr. Schmitt says that Chinese Communist Party can be held responsible, since it directed the actions of officials' (Dinan, 2020). While Schmitt is certainly right in recognizing the CPC's paramount power in China, he is certainly oblivious to the very origin and mission of the CPC: founded as an underground political organization within the international communist movement with an initial mission of anti-imperialism and anti-capitalism, the CPC has not been an ordinary bourgeoise political party with an incorporated legal status and registered address to which US courts can deliver their legal papers. The imperialists in Shanghai's French Concession where the CPC secretly initiated its founding event in 1921 would have to give this organization its registration paper in the first place in order for the CPC to be a legal entity to be charged. Thus, if the historical 'Boxer (Gengzi) Indemnity' in 1900 was truly tragic for the Chinese nation, this second call for the equivalent of a 'Gengzi Indemnity' in 2020 is truly farcical. Of course, those who initiated these domestic US lawsuits and international criminal court or human rights claims knew all too well that they were exploiting the Chinese for their own publicity gain while reinforcing a global symbolic environment of intimidation against China. COVID-19 finishes the perfect excuse for the unleashing of anti-communism as an ideological force.

Fang Fang's *Wuhan Diary* and the making of a transnational discursive alliance

Although the CPC gained Chinese state power through a widely supported revolution and Mao even waged a 'Cultural Revolution' with the intention to prevent a 'capitalist restoration' in post-revolutionary China, internal struggles over the future of China remain intense. As was the case with the Soviet Union (Saunders, 2013), anti-regime dissidents, in the most familiar embodiment of dissident writers, are the indispensable actors of a transnational anti-communist discursive formation. Overseas Chinese language media and media in the postcolonial city of Hong Kong produced some of the harshest indictments against the Chinese state over COVID-19. Initium Media, a Hong Kong-based outlet, for example, not only frames the Chinese state's response to the coronavirus as a failure of authoritarianism, but literally called the Chinese political system a 'virus' (Xin Bai, 27 February 2020, cited in Wang, 2020).

Within mainland China, the script casts the Wuhan-based female writer Fang Fang and her diaries. As a former chair of the Hubei Provincial Writers' Association, Fang Fang enjoys considerable official status and privileges. Yet, like many outspoken liberal intellectuals in China who are the darlings of Western media and scholarly circles, they have long internalized the West's dominant anti-communist perspective. This, after all, is exactly the state of an uneven discursive struggle over the future of China and by extension, the future of any struggle that posits communism as an alternative to capitalism. One of Fang Fang's well-known novels, entitled *Soft Burial*, is a harsh indictment against the CPC's historical land reform movement, which liberates the Chinese peasantry from an exploitative land ownership system. That such a novel was officially published in China in the first place was illustrative of the level of official tolerance for oppositional ideas.

Fang Fang, who was already in close contact with a US translator of her work before the outbreak of COVID-19, began to post her dairies on social media two days after Wuhan's lockdown on 23 January 2020. Combining her own lived experiences with unverified secondary sources as well as literary embellishments, and peppering her accounts with indictments against official incapacity and sensationalist depictions of 'funeral parlors full of mobile phones', her 60-entry diary, which ended on 24 March 2020, instantly grabbed national and global attention and served as a perfect

Wuhan-based first-person narrative for the global construction of an anti-communist COVID-19 discourse. The *Los Angeles Times* featured Fang Fang in a front page article under the title of 'Wuhan's voice of truth' (Su, 2020), while *The Diplomat* praised her as 'the conscience of Wuhan' (Adlakha, 2020). By 8 April 2020, her diary had been repackaged as *The Wuhan Diary*, with its English version available for pre-order and to be published by commercial publishers in the UK and Germany.

The swift production of Fang Fang's diary reveals a transnational discursive alliance in action. Roughly, it consists of the following key components: regime critics and their vocal supporters in Chinese social media outlets, universities, market-oriented media outlets; anti-communist Chinese language media outlets in Hong Kong, Taiwan, and the Chinese diaspora, Western government broadcast outlets, Western news agencies and mainstream media, Western academics who serve as translators, promoters and researchers of chosen Chinese authors, publishing houses with historical records as the commercial arm of a US-government led 'cultural Cold War' against communism. At the top of this discursive formation sits a whole set of award-giving and status-confirming institutions crowned by the Nobel Literary Prize or, in an even more politicized form, the Nobel Peace Prize. Unfortunately for Fang Fang and her supporters, and perhaps underscoring the point that other people's lived experience also matters in the discursive struggles for competing versions of reality, *The Wuhan Diary* did not fare well among the Chinese public, let alone the transnational reading public. The harsh situation of COVID-19 related injustice and suffering in the US, widely reported by the Chinese media and intimately experienced by overseas Chinese, made what Fang Fang depicted in Wuhan a prelude to just how bad things can be outside China. Furthermore, in a development that is highly ironic for Fang Fang and her supporters, her diary and its swift and seamless incorporation into the transnational anti-China discursive formation ended up providing a perfect opportunity for the Chinese polity to debate the existing state of the Chinese and global symbolic environments both online and offline. Instead of gaining popularity and exerting influence, the anti-China and anti-communist transnational discursive alliance lost much of its credibility and influence. In fact, racist and anti-communist discourses backfire in China, boosting the Chinese public's allegiance to the CPC and its confidence in the Chinese political system. In the end, Fang Fang, the Western media and Donald Trump ended up achieving what the CPC propaganda department could have only dreamed of by serving as a negative example.

Concluding remarks

There is no question that COVID-19 has hit those already on the margins of the global racial capitalist social order the hardest. In China, small shopkeepers, migrant workers and service sector workers had suffered disproportionately (Huang, 2020). However, as this chapter has tried to show, a fuller understanding of injustices engendered in the global struggles against COVID-19 must include a geopolitical and geo-cultural dimension that takes into account the production of an intersecting racist and anti-communist discursive formation aimed at China, a country that was the original 'epicentre' of the pandemic but soon became one of the world's safest countries precisely because the Chinese state has the political will, organizational capacity, a combined modern and traditional medical knowledge regime, as well as popular support to wage one of the most robust and best organized campaigns against COVID-19.

Our purpose, however, is not simply to depict China as a victim. Instead, it is to drive home this point: so long as China continues to be the West's racist and anti-communist 'Other' with all its real and imagined crimes, the door for a radical transformation of the racial capitalist formation will remain more difficult to open up. Socialism or barbarism – this remains the choice for humanity. The uneven nature of the global fight against COVID-19 has only reinforced the necessity of such a choice. As 'China's Chernobyl' turned into the 'West's Waterloo', and as Fang Fang and likeminded Chinese admirers of the US as the leading light of freedom and democracy became the laugh stock of China's increasingly self-confident public, including many among China's young netizens, we are left with many questions.

For the world community outside China, especially those who are committed to promoting transcultural justice and equality, we may ask: now that the weaponization of COVID-19 against China has lost its efficacy and even backfired, what's next? Who will benefit from the continuing sustenance of a transnational racist and anti-communist discursive formation against China? How can anti-racist justice and equality seekers in the West move beyond their own unreflective complicity in unwittingly accepting mainstream discourses against China? For China, a crucial challenge will be how to turn negative attacks and hostile external environments into opportunities for enlightened self-education, critical self-reflection, and concerted action aiming at building a more just, equal and ecologically sustainable domestic social order while contributing to a more just and peaceful post-racial and post-imperialist global order.

Note

[1] Dr Shi Zhengli is a scientist at the Wuhan Institute of Virology who had collaborated with US scientists in studying coronaviruses in bats.

References

Adlakha, H. (2020) 'Fang Fang: the "conscience of Wuhan" amid coronavirus quarantine', *The Diplomat*, 23 March. https://thed iplomat.com/2020/03/fang-fang-the-conscience-of-wuhan-amid-coronavirus-quarantine/

Chiacu, D. (2020) 'Coronavirus "cover-up" is China's Chernobyl – White House adviser', *Reuters*, 24 May. www.reuters.com/arti cle/healt-coronavirus-usa-china-idUSKBN23106X

Connolly, A. (2020) 'Coronavirus coverup is "China's Chernobyl moment," warn 100 politicians, experts', *The Global News*, 14 April. https://globalnews.ca/news/6814940/china-coronavi rus-open-letter/

Dinan, S. (2020) 'Missouri sues Chinese Communist Party for "billions of dollars" in coronavirus costs', *The Washington Times*, 21 April. www.washingtontimes.com/news/2020/apr/21/misso uri-sues-chinese-communist-party-billions-dol/

Fan, L. (2020) 'Absurd to sue China for virus', *China Daily*, 25 April. www.chinadaily.com.cn/a/202004/25/WS5ea3a4a7a310a8b24 115185a.html

Finnegan, C. (2020) 'Pompeo pushes "Wuhan virus" label to counter Chinese disinformation', *ABC News*, 25 March. https://abcn ews.go.com/Politics/pompeo-pushes-wuhan-virus-label-coun ter-chinese-disinformation/story?id=69797101

Huang, Y. (2020) 'Supporting SMEs to overcome the impact of the epidemic', *People's Daily*, 8 June. http://opinion.people.com.cn/ GB/n1/2020/0608/c1003-31738052.html.

Lim, D. (2019) 'The US, China and "Technology War"', *Global Asia*, 14(1): 8–13.

Mead, W.R. (2020) 'China is the real sick man of Asia', *The Wall Street Journal*, 3 February. www.wsj.com/articles/china-is-the- real-sick-man-of-asia-11580773677

Nair, R. (2020) 'Vancouver's Chinatown lions defaced by racist graffiti for second time', *CBC News*, 29 May. www.cbc.ca/news/ canada/british-columbia/lions-defaced-again-1.5591382

Quinn, M. (2020) 'Conservative lawyer sues Chinese government over coronavirus outbreak', *CBC News*, 19 March. www.cbsnews. com/news/coronavirus-lawyer-larry-klayman-sues-chinese-gov ernment-over-outbreak/

Ritter, K. (2020) 'Lawsuit: China hid virus information, should pay billions', *US News & World Report*, 24 March. www.usnews.com/news/best-states/nevada/articles/2020-03-24/lawsuit-china-hid-virus-information-should-pay-billions

Saunders, F. S. (2013) *The Cultural Cold War: The CIA and the World of Arts and Letters*. The New Press.

Su, A. (2020) 'Two months into coronavirus lockdown, her online diary is a window into life and death in Wuhan', *The Los Angeles Times*, 21 March. www.latimes.com/world-nation/story/2020-03-21/china-wuhan-coronavirus-diary-fang-fang

Tan, H. (2020) 'China "owes us": Growing outrage over Beijing's handling of the coronavirus pandemic', *CNBC*, 22 April. www.cnbc.com/2020/04/24/lawsuits-outrage-over-chinas-handling-of-the-coronavirus-pandemic.html

Tharoor, I. (2020) 'China's Chernobyl? The coronavirus outbreak leads to a loaded metaphor', *The Washington Post*, 11 February. www.washingtonpost.com/world/2020/02/12/chinas-chernobyl-coronavirus-outbreak-leads-loaded-metaphor/

Tracy, M. (2020) 'Inside *The Wall Street Journal*, tensions rise over "sick man" China Headline', *The New York Times*, 22 February. www.nytimes.com/2020/02/22/business/media/wall-street-journal-sick-man-china-headline.html?_ga=2.148771765.345894699.1608949920-366020462.1608949920

Trofimov, Y. (2020) 'From Chernobyl to the Coronavirus; In the U.S.S.R. in 1986, as in China today, a public health disaster exposed the limits of dictatorial rule', *The Wall Street Journal*, 13 February. www.wsj.com/articles/from-chernobyl-to-the-coronavirus-11581610088

Tyler, O. (2020) 'Class-action suit seeks to bill China for coronavirus fallout: "We want the court to make them pay"', *Fox News*, 25 March. www.foxnews.com/politics/class-action-suit-seeks-to-make-china-pay

Wang, D. (2020) 'Prejudice, discrimination, and the immunology paradigm: a critical discourse analysis of the New York Times' reports on the respective responses to Covid-19 by China and Italy'. Simon Fraser University.

Ward, S. (2019) 'Because China isn't "Caucasian," the U.S. is planning for a "clash of civilizations." That could be dangerous.' *Washington Post*, 4 May. www.washingtonpost.com/politics/2019/05/04/because-china-isnt-caucasian-us-is-planning-clash-civilizations-that-could-be-dangerous/

Xin B. (2020), Feb. 27). 'Virus, revolution and authoritarian: The politics of Chinese Virus'/病毒、革命和极权：中国病毒的政治学. *Theinitium*/端传媒（简体）. https://theinitium.com/article/20200227-opinion-china-virus-resistance/

Young, I. (2020) '"Disgusting" Attacker punches Asian women in the face in Vancouver, amid spate of racist hate crimes', *South China Morning Post*, 6 May. www.scmp.com/news/world/united-states-canada/article/3083015/disgusting-attacker-punches-asian-woman-face

Zhao, Y. (2014) 'The life and times of "Chimerica": Global press discourses on U.S.-China economic integration, financial crisis, and power shifts', *International Journal of Communication*, (8): 419–44.

Zheng, L. (2019) 'Clash of civilization' narrative dangerous, *China Daily*, 27 May. www.chinadaily.com.cn/kindle/2019-05-27/content_37474201.htm

FOUR

Life or Livelihood? COVID-19 in the UK and the Existential Question of Our Times

Radha D'Souza[1]

Introduction

COVID-19 presents the UK with the impossible choice of prioritizing lives or livelihoods, putting the government between 'a rock and a hard place'. This dilemma raises important questions about the disconnect between the economy and social identities of individuals and communities – a disconnect that is institutionalized by labour market regulation on the one hand and non-discrimination laws on the other. My aim for this chapter is to problematize the disconnect. I do this by juxtaposing developments in the UK labour markets since the neoliberal reforms first initiated in the 1980s by Margaret Thatcher and successive race relations legislation that accompanied the reforms and was later codified as the Equality Act 2010. My objective is to highlight the paradoxical nature of the two simultaneous processes, one related to the UK economy and the other to a society comprised of individuals, communities, and the Welsh, Scottish and Irish nations. Paradoxes signal a knowledge gap. In this case they signal a gap in knowledge about the relationship between deregulation of labour market and strengthening of laws on equality and non-discrimination.

COVID-19 invites us to reconsider the theoretical and conceptual frameworks within which work and labour rights on the one hand, and equality and non-discrimination on the other, are understood. The disconnect between economy and polity has been theorized in political economy literature especially in Marxist political economy (for example, Nitzan and Bichler, 2000; Wood, 1995). COVID-19 pushes us to think deeper about the role of law in liberal societies in establishing and reproducing relationships of social marginalization in the economy (D'Souza, 2018).

In this chapter I examine how the law frames approaches to the big question that COVID-19 presents to the UK government and policy makers namely: life or livelihood? These frameworks and concepts continue to remain embedded within philosophical liberalism in law and in politics that no longer work as the 'life or livelihood?' challenge posed by COVID-19 demonstrates. I argue that delinking economy and society, a handiwork of liberal legal systems, gives with one hand what it takes away with the other for marginalized communities. The life or livelihood dilemma must be located within the disjuncture between economy and society that characterizes liberal capitalist societies such as the UK.

Three levels of marginalization: the context for COVID-19 in the UK

A point of departure for this volume on the impact of COVID-19 on marginalized communities, could be to ask how marginalization was perceived in the UK. Perceptions of marginalization operated at three levels: individual and group, national, and sub-national. Together these perceptions of marginalization shaped discourses about COVID-19 and post-COVID-19 economic recovery plans.

Marginalization: individual and community level

At the level of the individual, the meaning of 'marginalized communities' was shaped by the Equality Act 2010. The Equality Act 2010 was a watershed moment when equality impact assessments of state policies and non-discrimination became statutory duties for decision makers in the public and private sectors. The Equality Act 2010 protects certain social groups that possess what are called 'protected characteristics' in the Act. The Act protects people with 'protected characteristics' from direct and indirect discrimination, harassment and victimization. 'Protected characteristics' include age, disability, gender reassignment, marriage and civil partnership, pregnancy and maternity, race, religion or belief, sex, and sexual orientation. Thus, individual identities are the basis for protections under the Equality Act 2010. Individual identities are also the basis for recognizing social groups as 'communities'. Individuals with 'protected characteristics' are perceived as 'marginalized' and groups of individuals with each protected characteristic is perceived as a 'marginalized community'.

The Equality Act 2010 informed how data was collected and from the outset structured perceptions of marginalization as well as the discourse on social impact of COVID-19. Unlike in some countries, data and information on how the pandemic disproportionately impacted marginalized communities was never lacking in the UK. Very early on in the pandemic, campaign groups, professional organizations, academic research funding bodies, scholarly communities, government agencies, the national statistical agencies and other organizations launched studies and published reports on the disproportionate impact of COVID-19 on marginalized communities. Social sciences and humanities were out there in the research from the outset, and not as a belated appendage to medical sciences, as was the case in the past. Recently the British Academy published what is to date the most comprehensive study, titled *The COVID Decade: Understanding the Long-Term Societal Impacts of COVID-19* (The British Academy, 2021a), together with a companion report – *Shaping The COVID Decade: Addressing the Long-Term Societal Impacts of COVID-19* (The British Academy, 2021b) – that addresses policy recommendations. The British Academy report was commissioned by the Government Office for Science to provide an independent review of the societal impacts of COVID-19.

The report confirmed what was widely known: that COVID-19 exacerbated pre-existing structural inequalities in British society and accelerated existing trends; that sustained cutbacks to public spending on health, education and social services over four decades had left many marginalized communities vulnerable; that low-paid jobs and wealth disparities had increased as had queues at food banks. The British Academy report is at pains to highlight the differential impacts along dimensions of race, ethnicity, gender, sexuality, age, abilities, and immigration status. The report was also clear that the impact of COVID-19 was going to be long term and likely to last a decade or more. What is interesting in the British Academy report and indeed numerous other reports on COVID-19 is that while the empirical data and analysis has emphasized the disproportionate impact of COVID-19 on marginalized communities these reports leave us with the question: 'and now, what next?'. Individual identity as defined under the Equality Act 2010 as the basis for non-discrimination and community formation invites questions about the meaning of identity and community in theory and their connections to the economy, in particular the labour market.

Marginalization: national level

Turning to the wider national context, COVID-19 struck the UK when there was heightened angst about marginalization at national level that added another layer to the marginalization at individual and community levels. The impact of COVID-19 on marginalized UK communities unfolded against the backdrop of Brexit. The UK had just formally exited the European Union on 1 January 2020 when COVID-19 was declared a global pandemic by the WHO. Here, perceptions of marginalization were shaped by another kind of law: parliamentary sovereignty in the UK constitution. The legal necessity to negotiate a complex trade deal with the EU by the end of 31 December 2020 shadowed responses to the pandemic throughout the year. The campaign to leave the EU was driven by a sense that the UK was marginalized within the EU. Indeed, during the Leave campaign, the current prime minister Boris Johnson, repeatedly claimed that Britain risked becoming a 'satellite state' within the EU (Read, 2018). The Brexit campaign promised that 'sovereign' UK would seek trade deals with other nations around the world that would put the UK on the road to prosperity again. The downturn in economies of countries around the world in the wake of COVID-19 put a question mark on hopes for expansion of trade internationally. These ambitions were scuppered by another kind of marginalization that is known but rarely spoken about.

The UK state as a political institution is inextricably entwined with the US state's giant military-industrial-technology complex. A maze of multiple defence, security, intelligence sharing agreements, extradition treaties, arms production and sale, revolving doors between defence personnel and the US defence establishment and much else makes the UK state politically already a 'satellite state' of the US, politely referred to as the 'special relationship' (also see Baylis, 1981; Edgerton, 2005; Private Eye, 2016). The anti-China, anti-Iran drumbeats in the US played out as COVID-19 unfolded. The economic necessity to seek trade with countries outside the EU and political necessity of maintaining the 'special relationship', pulled the economy in different directions even as COVID-19 decimated the economy and the state's capacities for manoeuvre (Donnelly, 2020; Parker, 2021). None of these issues informed post-COVID-19 recovery strategies for marginalized communities even though it is widely believed that they are bound to shape the recovery in multiple ways.

Marginalization: sub-national level

Turning from risks of marginalization of the UK internationally, to sub-national ones, another kind of law – the terms of devolution and fears of erosion of autonomy for the devolved nations – shaped perceptions of marginalization of the different nations constitutive of the UK. The pre-pandemic relations between the nations of the UK were already at its lowest point as a result of Brexit. Scotland, Northern Ireland, and Wales, nations that see themselves as marginalized within the United Kingdom, emerged from the Brexit campaign feeling even more marginalized. The three nations saw Brexit as economically disadvantageous to them. COVID-19 fuelled those sentiments as the UK government struggled to respond to the pandemic.

Critical of the UK government's centralized responses, all three nations charted their own strategies to combat the pandemic. These responses of marginalized nations fed into strident demands for independence in Scotland (Small, 2021), it reopened tensions between unionists and republicans in Northern Ireland (Hearty, 2021), and Welsh nationalism gained ground, by an estimated 39 per cent, as the Welsh Assembly acquired new confidence as it charted its own course out of the pandemic (ITV, 2021). The UK passed the Internal Market Act 2020 to further centralize economic powers and integrate internal markets after Brexit, for which the Scottish and Welsh parliaments refused consent (Institute for Government, n.d.). The British Academy report (2021b) notes that whereas community solidarities and cohesion increased at local and hyper-local levels during the pandemic, regional, sub-national and national solidarities decreased.

At all three levels, the law, public law at that, shaped conceptions of marginalization. Yet, policy research and responses largely focused on just one: marginalization shaped by the Equality Act 2010. What is notable about these perceptions and public discourses about the pathway out of the pandemic is that changes to wages, working conditions, and unionization were at best on the margins in the debates on solutions, mostly as rhetorical affirmations of job oriented post-Brexit, post-pandemic recovery, as discussed in the next section.

Economy, society and COVID-19

The Equality Act 2010 was the culmination of decades of struggles by Black Asian and Ethnic Minority communities (BAME), women, people with disabilities and LGBTQ+ social groups for equal opportunities in employment and services. Marginalized communities argued that they were unable to compete in the labour market because of lack of social capital: health, education, skills, and opportunities. The Equality Act 2010 seeks to level the playing field for marginalized communities at policy level and in social practices. By doing so, the law aims to enable marginalized communities to compete as equals for jobs and services.

The protections to certain individuals and communities in the Equality Act 2010 are based on the assumption that there will be a relatively stable labour market, and that if individuals and communities with protected characteristics worked in low-paying, insecure jobs, it was because they were discriminated by employers or unable to access employment opportunities. Assumptions about availability of jobs provides the objective conditions within which equal opportunities for social groups with 'protected characteristics' plays out.

In the UK, the political trajectory of Equality Act 2010 paralleled an economic trajectory that introduced large-scale restructuring of UK economy and social services. Successive amendments to the Race Relations Act 1965 occurred alongside labour market restructuring and far-reaching liberalization and privatization of the economy. The Equality

Act 2010 consolidated the ad hoc amendments to the Race Relations Acts of the past into a single codified statute (Hand et al, 2012). Labour market restructuring brought with it deindustrialization, de-unionization and informalization of work, the most recent variant being the controversial 'zero hour' contracts. 'Zero hour' contracts are employment contracts that do not oblige employers to provide minimum hours of work, but nevertheless require contracted workers to be available for work when required. The number of people on 'zero hour' contracts increased from 896,000 in 2019 to 1.05 million in 2020 (Jeyaraj, 2020). Liberalization and privatization rolled back the state from public services and brought basic services like health, education and housing under market regimes and the private sector. Thus, what the Equality Act 2010 gave with one hand – equal access to jobs – it took away with the other – labour market restructuring – and liberalization and privatization of the economy that emphasized 'efficiencies' at work through retrenchment of workforce, contracting out work to destinations where labour costs were lower, and adopting 'jobless growth' strategies (Burton, 2014). For example, the disproportionate numbers of deaths in care homes during the pandemic put the spotlight on the privatization of care services that employed BAME women on lower than minimum wages and long working hours (Kelly, 2020). Paradoxical as it may appear, economic deprivation in marginalized communities increased after equality and non-discrimination laws for the majority while increasing individual social mobility for a few (Equalities and Human Rights Commission, 2015).

COVID-19 brought the economy to its knees and with it the labour market, a possibility that no economist had considered. The near collapse of the economy, considered by some to be the worst in 300 years, comes at a time when the UK stands at a historic crossroad where multiple levels of marginalization could impact the economy in ways that increase marginalization of those communities already on the margins, even when more stringent policies for equality and non-discrimination are put in place to mitigate the effects of COVID-19.

While recognizing the disproportionate impact of COVID-19 on marginalized communities, academics, policy makers and activists continue to seek solutions within existing liberal legal and market frameworks on which the very foundations of the UK social order rests, and the historical roots of which go down very deep. These frameworks do not address the structural disjuncture between economy and society: the hiatus between equality and non-discrimination laws in the legal frameworks on the one hand, and competitive labour markets in a deregulated economy on the other. The economic goals of free market economics in market liberalism and the political goals of redistributive justice in liberal democracies do not work in tandem. The moves to address the marginalization of individuals and communities with 'protected characteristics' remain largely within the 'free market' solutions to the far-reaching economic impacts of COVID-19. Brexit pushes these 'free market' solutions in the direction of intensifying the international competitiveness of the British economy, away from the redistributive justice thrust of the Equality Act 2010. The tensions between the direction of the national economy and their impacts on local communities and individuals feeds into fissiparous tendencies at sub-national level feeding fears of a 'Dis'United Kingdom.

The government continues to reaffirm that its economic recovery strategies will be centred around creating high quality, well-paying jobs (UK Government, 2021). Liberal democracies like the UK depend on corporations and businesses to create jobs, however. States must make their territories attractive to corporations and investors by lowering wages and environmental standards, reducing regulatory oversight, reducing taxation and supporting free movements of commodities and money. We are in a tautological loop here.

States must invest in social capital – health, education, housing and social care – if communities with 'protected characteristics' are to have equal opportunities in the labour markets. Being attractive to corporations and investors comes at the cost of the resources needed to build social capital. Corporations find territories with low wages and low environmental standards, minimum regulation and taxation and permissive movements of commodities and money more attractive as they reduce costs and increase profitability, which in turn reduces the resources for states to invest in working people. The need to make their territories attractive to corporations and investors generates a spiral of what economists have called 'regulatory competition' (in relation to labour standards, see Charny, 2000; in relation to regulation theory, see Jessop, 2015). Brexit opens up new opportunities for corporations to do two things: either relocate to other, cheaper friendlier locations or push the UK to reduce standards as trade-off for job creation, at lower wages and minimal regulation. We are back to square one.

Those most impacted by COVID-19 – those with 'protected characteristics' – will inevitably be the ones most under pressure to take up anything on offer in the job markets, including zero hour contracts with unlimited working hours at any wage at all. At the same time, the very promise of equality and non-discrimination will prompt people with 'protected characteristics' to compete in the labour market, on unfair terms if need be, in the hope they might succeed in 'climbing on to the job ladder' as it were. A ladder is not a ladder if it is not vertical. The verticality of the job market means that each step in the employment ladder can only accommodate a small number of persons on its steps at a given time. The majority must compete with all the rest, first to get on to the ladder, and then to stay there.

Interventions for equality and redistributive justice in liberal democracies argue for increasing opportunities for people with 'protected characteristics' through redistribution of tax and revenue incomes of the state more fairly but offer few solutions to building an economy that does not rely on corporations or investors or, at the least, suggest ways to build an economy that is resilient to corporate and investor diktats. Rather, progressive thinkers call for disciplining corporations and investors by using the state's regulatory power, while at the same time reiterating their commitment to liberal democracy in which property rights are equal if not superior to human rights (see D'Souza, 2018).

In a social order founded on economy–society dualism, the economic rationale of non-discrimination laws is often not recognized. The Equality Act 2010 creates what in free-trade-speak is called a 'level playing field'. 'Level playing fields' are an integral component of trade rules as they facilitate fair competition by equalizing the playing field for corporations and investors. The equalizing measures include social standards, which encompass labour standards, such as wages and working conditions (see D'Souza, 2018). Post-COVID-19 economic recovery strategies do not bridge the two parallel trajectories of economic and social developments which are considered independently in insular ways. The British Academy reports (2021a, 2021b), for example, did not consider economic reforms at all when recommending social policies supportive of marginalized communities.

Class is not a 'protected characteristic' under the Equality Act 2010. Conceptually, class is related to labour and work. Labour, or the human capacity to work, has dual aspects. On the one hand it is an economic category and commodity. As a saleable commodity labour is bought and sold in the labour markets. In economic theory markets are price fixing mechanisms where buyers and sellers agree to sale and purchase of any commodity including labour. Trade unions and collective bargaining seek to increase the price of labour whereas employer associations adopt a range of strategies to reduce it including mechanization, contracting out and relocating production to cheaper destinations. The law permits both processes to enable labour markets to find the appropriate market price for labour.

Labour is also the working class – a social group categorized according to their wealth and income status as lower in the social hierarchy. Labour markets trade in abstract labour, labour that is stripped of specific attributes of race, religion, colour, gender, nationality. As a commodity it is simply the capacity to work that is bought and sold. However, labour as a social class is never abstract. All persons with capacities to work must necessarily exist with a variety of social attributes – they must be of some colour, gender, race, religion, linguistic group, nationality. There is no worker or employee who does not have some kind of gender, race, nationality or other identities. It is significant therefore that the Equality Act 2010 paralleled labour market restructuring, and liberalization and privatization. Understanding the causal connections between the two processes, both operationalized by law, will be the key to reimagining another kind of intervention in the social restructuring that will inevitably follow COVID-19.

Envisioning a post-COVID-19 future

Given the three tiers of marginalization, at individual/community, national, and sub-national levels, what can we say about the impact of COVID-19 on marginalized communities in the UK?

Historically, pandemics, like wars, have invariably led to structural social change (Cummins et al, 2013). The nature of these changes depends on the capacities of communities to rethink and re-envision structural changes in society. For example, during the World Wars different sections in liberal capitalist societies re-imagined the world in three different ways: social welfarism as a model for a more humane capitalism; fascism as a model for a strong nation; and socialism as a model for a non–capitalist society. These reimaginations were critical in shaping the structural changes that emerged after the end of the World Wars. What is unfolding before us today is at least a decade or more of social and economic restructuring and change. Are marginalized communities able to radically reimagine a different social order based on fairness, dignity and justice?

The extensive empirical studies, investigations and policy interventions since the outbreak of the pandemic accept the social architecture established by liberal capitalism as given, almost as a natural condition of social life. Liberal capitalism rests on the institutional separation of economy and society. Law establishes these institutions and manages the hiatus between economy and society. The Equality Act 2010 exemplifies the hiatus between economy and society.

Can critical scholars and activists in the UK take a root and branch approach that seeks to rebuild a post-COVID-19 society in which the economy and society go hand in hand and reimagine a political economy in which building social capital for marginalized communities and labour market competition do not cancel out the other? This is the challenge that COVID-19 presents to the marginalized communities in the UK. Are lives and livelihoods both possible in a post-COVID-19 future?

Note

[1] I wish to thank Nehmat Kaur who worked as research assistant on this project.

References

Baylis, J. (1981) *Anglo-American Defence Relations 1939–1984: The Special Relationship*. Macmillan.

Burton, B. (2014) 'Neoliberalism and the Equality Act 2010: a missed opportunity for gender justice?', *Industrial Law Journal*, 43(2): 122–48.

Charny, D. (2000) 'Regulatory competition and the global coordination of labor standards', *Journal of International Economic Law*, 3(2): 281–302. doi:10.1093/jiel/3.2.281

Cummins, N., Kelly, M. and Gráda, C.Ó. (2013) 'Living standards and plague in London, 1560–1665', *Centre for Economic Research Working Paper Series*, No. WP13/08. UCD School of Economics, University College Dublin.

D'Souza, R. (2018) *What's Wrong With Rights? Social Movements, Law and Liberal Imaginations*, Pluto Press.

Donnelly, D. (2020) 'Brexit shock: How tensions between USA and China may affect UK's trade options', *The Express*, 9 June.

Edgerton, D. (2005) *Warfare State: Britain, 1920–1970*, Cambridge University Press.

Equalities and Human Rights Commission, UK (2015) Is Britain Fairer? The State of Equality and Human Rights 2015. www.equalityhumanrights.com/en/publication-download/britain-fairer-2015

Hand, J., Davis, B. and Feast, P. (2012) 'Unification, simplification, amplification? An analysis of aspects of the British Equality Act 2010', *Commonwealth Law Bulletin*, 38(3): 509–28.

Hearty, K. (2021) 'How COVID has reopened sectarian tensions over policing in Northern Ireland', *The Conversation*, 10 February. https://theconversation.com/how-covid-has-reopened-sectarian-tensions-over-policing-in-northern-ireland-154895

Institute for Government (n.d.) 'UK Internal Market Act'. www.instituteforgovernment.org.uk/explainers/internal-market-act

ITV (2021) 'Poll reveals highest support for Welsh independence ever recorded', 4 March. www.itv.com/news/wales/2021-03-04/poll-reveals-highest-support-for-welsh-independence-ever-recorded

Jessop, B. (2015) 'The course, contradictions, and consequences of extending competition as a mode of (meta-) governance: towards a sociology of competition and its limits', *Distinktion: Journal of Social Theory*, 16(2), 167–85.

Jeyaraj, P. (2020) 'Zero hours worker numbers now top 1 million – driven by increasing numbers of Covid 19 key workers', 21 March. www.zerohoursjustice.org/blog/zero-hours-worker-numbers-now-top-1-million-driven-by-increasing-numbers-of-covid-19-key-workers

Kelly, E. (2020) 'Social care and the COVID-19 pandemic', *Institute for Fiscal Studies* (IFS), 3 July. https://ifs.org.uk/publications/14923

Nitzan, J. and Bichler, S. (2000) 'Capital accumulation: breaking the dualism of 'economics' and 'politics', in R. Palan (ed), *Global Political Economy: Contemporary Theories* (pp 67–88), Routledge.

Parker, G. (2021) 'UK calls for world to 'get tough' with China as part of global trade shake-up', *Financial Times*, 30 March.

Private Eye (2016) *Revolving Doors Special Report: Public Servants, Private Paydays*. www.private-eye.co.uk/pictures/special_reports/revolving-doors.pdf

Read, C. (2018) 'Brexit warning: Boris says "historic mistake" will see UK become a "satellite state"', *The Express*, 24 November.

Small, M. (2021) 'A post-Covid Scotland must be a post-UK Scotland', *Bella Caledonia*, 24 January. https://bellacaledonia.org.uk/2021/01/24/a-post-covid-scotland-must-be-a-post-british-scotland/

The British Academy (2021a) *The COVID Decade: Understanding the Long-Term Societal Impacts of COVID-19*. www.thebritishacademy.ac.uk/publications/covid-decade-understanding-the-long-term-societal-impacts-of-covid-19/

The British Academy (2021b) *Shaping the COVID Decade: Addressing the Long-Term Societal Impacts of COVID-19*. www.thebritishacademy.ac.uk/publications/shaping-the-covid-decade-addressing-the-long-term-societal-impacts-of-covid-19/

UK Government (2021) 'Build Back Better: our plan for growth', 3 March. www.gov.uk/government/publications/build-back-better-our-plan-for-growth/build-back-better-our-plan-for-growth-html

Wood, E.M. (1995) *Democracy Against Capitalism: Renewing Historical Materialism*, Cambridge University Press.

FIVE

Understanding Barriers and Facilitators to Genomic Research Participation Among Minority Populations: A Piloted Community Survey in Flint, MI

Mieka Smart, Megan Mulheron, Yvonne Nong, Crystal Juarez, Emiko Blalock, Roland J. Thorpe Jr, and Amanda Woodward

Acknowledgements

The authors wish to acknowledge the project's funding source, the National Institutes of Health, Grant P30 AG01528, and the following individuals whose efforts contributed to the success of this project: Jessica Gutierrez and Neletha Skelton.

Background and introduction

In Flint, Michigan, US, residents have been dealing with a wide range of psychosocial and health-related consequences that include government mistrust due to valid experiences of being marginalized by structural racism and classism, and trauma-related responses (Fortenberry et al, 2018). Therefore, maximizing racially representative participation in public health research or interventions may be especially challenging in Flint, where residents have become deeply distrustful and sceptical of the motives of those connected to both government and academic institutions (Cuthbertson et al, 2016). For many, COVID-19 is reminiscent of the recent fatality-causing drinking water crisis in Flint, as it evokes similar feelings of mistrust in the government's ability to protect the public from health-related disasters (Sneed et al, 2020).

In the context of the COVID-19 vaccine trials, recent studies have examined barriers to participation among minority populations. Ekezie and colleagues (2021) found that there was agreement across ethnicities that clinical research was necessary, but many were wary of visiting hospitals for vaccine trials that required physical examinations or blood tests. Additionally, language differences, fears (of contracting the virus, side effects, or lack of support if complications arose) and suspicion of hidden agendas behind the vaccine were also noted as barriers to participation (Ekezie et al, 2021).

Minority populations, particularly Black adults, have expressed greater reservations about receiving the COVID-19 vaccine compared with White adults (Artiga et al, 2021). Studies have revealed that minority apprehensions towards getting the COVID-19 vaccine were due to mistrust in both the medical establishment and the government, accelerated development of the vaccine, limited data on side effects and safety, and a racially unjust political environment (Momplaisir et al, 2021; Nguyen et al, 2021). These findings are consistent with a Pew Research Center survey that was distributed in April and May 2020, in which 54 per cent of Black adults reported that they would definitely or probably get a COVID-19 vaccine compared with 74 per cent of White and Hispanic adults (Jaklevic, 2020). It is reasonable to infer that minority hesitation to participate in the COVID-19 vaccine trials is associated with barriers similar to those found in minority willingness to participate in research overall (Durant et al, 2014). Scepticism, stories of prior abuse at the hands of the government (for example, the US Public Health Service

Tuskegee Syphilis Experiment), and language divides were all likely barriers that affect minority recruitment efforts.

For minority participants, more contemporary issues guide health care decision making. Currently, the US is the only major developed economy that does not offer free healthcare to its citizens (Bodenheimer and Grumbach, 2016). The existing economic model allows individuals with more income to purchase quality specialized care, while marginalized individuals with less income get lower quality, less specialized healthcare. Currently, Black and Latinx communities have had difficulty accessing the COVID-19 vaccine due to loopholes allowing more affluent individuals to obtain those appointments (Dembosky, 2021). This idea corroborates findings from the Tuskegee Legacy Project, where Black and White adults were equally willing to participate in biomedical research, while Blacks were 1.8 times more likely to report a greater level of fear from participating in said research (Katz et al, 2006). This suggests that a purposeful, anti-racist approach is needed.

As for facilitators to participation, stakeholders have emphasized that establishing rapport with communities could help to promote minority participation in research (Durant et al, 2014). Recruitment efforts could also be improved by referring all patients to pertinent clinical trials, even if they are not eligible, and encouraging external referrals (Durant et al, 2014). Other studies have found that if participation addresses a health concern that is personally relevant or has the potential to benefit future generations, respondents may be more inclined to engage in the research process (McDonald et al, 2014; De Vries et al, 2016; Fisher et al, 2020).

Estimates of how genomic participation rates differ between Black and White populations are few, and there is currently limited qualitative research that examines why racial disparities in genomic research participation persist (McQuillan et al, 2003; McQuillan et al, 2006). Furthermore, research aimed at understanding how to rebuild trust and increase minority participation is minimal. This work is important because it can help to clarify reasons for hesitancy among minority populations to participate in other public health efforts during crises like the COVID-19 pandemic.

Methods

Overview

Throughout September 2019, we deployed the Barriers and Facilitators to Genomic Research Participation Survey at three community events in Flint, Michigan.

Study population

The study population was designed to include adult residents of Flint (18+) who were attending community events.

Individuals who chose to participate completed a brief, 34-question survey. From start to finish, survey completion took approximately 15 minutes. Respondents who completed the survey received a single, randomized incentive valued between US$1 and US$40.

Survey

The survey deployed consisted of seven domains: demographics, research attitudes, privacy concerns, perceived discrimination, institutional trust, financial wellness, and willingness to participate.

Five questions were included to obtain demographic information about respondents, including their gender, ethnicity, race, education level, and employment status. To measure research attitudes, the Research Attitudes Questionnaire (RAQ) was utilized. The RAQ is an 11-question scale with five Likert options (Rubright et al, 2011). To evaluate privacy concerns, two items were presented in the survey. Questions asked respondents if they believed that unauthorized personnel would view their personal information, and whether they believed their genetic material would end up in a police database if they chose to participate.

To assess perceived discrimination, five items were included in the survey. In the first four, respondents indicated how often they experienced the following events: being treated with less respect than others, receiving poorer service than others, people thinking of them as unintelligent, and people perceiving them as threatening. Then respondents were asked to consider whether events they reported were discriminatory based on race, ethnicity, ancestry, national origin, sex, age, or other.

Institutional trust was examined by way of three survey questions. Respondents were asked to report how often they believed the following groups would do what is morally right: the national government, the state government, and our own academic research institution.

To measure financial wellness, respondents were asked to rank how well they felt they could afford their basic needs (housing, food, utilities, transportation, health care) with their current income.

Each participant was asked to rank their likelihood of participating in a study based on one of seven randomly assigned health research scenarios. Each scenario started with the same two sentences: 'Imagine you were asked to participate in a health research project in Flint. One of the goals of the project would be to determine how people's genes interact with their environment to affect their future health.' For each scenario, the third sentence contained information about the factor being studied, prefaced by the words 'If you agreed to participate …':

- Factor 1 (Genomics): '… the information collected from this study would go towards advancing genomics research.'
- Factor 2 (Returning research results): '… researchers would be required to provide you with the results found from this study.'

- Factor 3 (Involvement of the entire family): '... we would interview every member of your home above the age of 5.'
- Factor 4 (Venous blood specimen donation): '... you'd be asked to give a small tube of blood so that researchers could analyze your genes.'
- Factor 5 (Blood spot donation): '... you'd be asked to give a small spot of blood so that researchers could analyze your genes.'
- Factor 6 (Longitudinal research participation): '... you'd be taking part in a longitudinal, or long-term, study that would require participation now and at several time points in the future.'
- Factor 7 (Interview location): '... the interview process would take place in your home.'

Respondents were then asked to explain why they ranked their likelihood of participating in the specific scenario they were assigned the way that they did.

Results

Across the three community events, 42 potential participants were approached. In total, 41 completed the survey, resulting in a 97.6 per cent response rate. Of the 41 respondents, 80.5 per cent reported being female. With respect to race and ethnicity, 87.8 per cent of respondents reported not being of Hispanic, Latino or Spanish origin. Additionally, the sample population consisted of 78.1 per cent Black or African American respondents (see Table 5.1).

For the highest level of education attained, 12.2 per cent completed 11th grade, 17.1 per cent completed 12th grade but did not receive a diploma, 24.4 per cent earned their high school degree, and 46.3 per cent received at least some college education (see Table 5.1).

For employment status, 26.9 per cent of respondents were either employed for wages or self-employed, 43.8 per cent were unemployed, and 29.3 per cent were retired (see Table 5.1).

Table 5.1: Respondent demographics

Survey question	Frequency (%) $n = 41$
Gender	
Male	7 (17.1)
Female	33 (80.5)
Refused	1 (2.4)
Hispanic, Latino or Spanish origin	
No	36 (87.8)
Yes	3 (7.3)
Refused	2 (4.9)
Race	
Black or African American	32 (78.1)
White	6 (14.6)
American Indian/Alaskan Native and Black	2 (4.9)
Don't know	1 (2.4)
Highest level of education attained	
11th grade	5 (12.2)
12th grade, no diploma	7 (17.1)
High school graduate	10 (24.4)
Some college, no degree	11 (26.8)
Associate degree, occup, tech, voc	2 (4.9)
Associate degree, academic programme	1 (2.4)
Bachelor's degree	4 (9.8)
Master's degree	1 (2.4)
Employment status	
Currently employed for wages	9 (22.0)
Self-employed	2 (4.9)
Receiving disability wages	6 (14.6)
Out of work for less than 1 year	2 (4.9)
Homemaker	3 (7.3)
College student	1 (2.4)
Retired	12 (29.3)
Never had a job	3 (7.3)
Unable to work	3 (7.3)

In the domain drawing from the RAQ, respondents generally responded 'neutral' to 'agree' (3 and 4 on a 5-point scale, respectively). However, for two items, respondents felt more strongly. For the statement 'modern science does more harm than good', respondents fell between 'disagree' and 'neutral' with a mean score of 2.85. Additionally, respondents agreed more strongly with the statement 'medical research needs to be closely regulated in order to prevent harm to research participants' (mean = 4.05) (see Table 5.2).

With respect to privacy concerns, when respondents were asked 'if you enrolled in research, tell us how worried you would be that someone not authorized would see your private information', they, on average, reported being more worried than not (mean = 3.27). Similarly, for the question, 'if a research project collected your genetic information, how worried would you be that it might end up in a police database', respondents again reported being more worried than not (mean = 3.56) (see Table 5.2).

For statements concerning government and institutional trust, respondents expressed that they could trust the government in Washington to do what is right 'some of the time' (mean = 3.25), and that they could trust both the Michigan state government and researchers at our university to do what is right 'most of the time' (mean = 2.98 and mean = 2.44, respectively).

In the domain addressing financial wellness, 38 valid responses were recorded. On average, respondents felt that they could meet their basic needs 'somewhat well' with their current income (mean = 2.34) (see Table 5.2).

With regards to willingness to take part in one of the seven randomly assigned health research scenarios, findings demonstrated that individuals were more willing than not to participate (mean = 3.34) (see Table 5.2).

When assessing respondents' rationale for perceived discrimination, 34.1 per cent felt that their 'race, ethnicity, ancestry, or national origin' were the main reasons for these

Table 5.2: Mean responses for the Barriers and Facilitators to Research Participation Survey

Research Attitudes Questionnaire	Mean response (scale 1–5) 1 = Strongly disagree 5 = Strongly agree	SD
Survey responses (n)	41	–
I have a positive view about medical research in general	3.51	1.23
Medical researchers are mainly motivated by personal gain	3.24	1.14
Medical researchers can be trusted to protect the interests of the people who take part in their research studies	3.37	0.99
We all have some responsibility to help others by volunteering for medical research	3.63	1.11
Modern science does more harm than good	2.85	0.96
Society needs to devote more resources to medical research	3.93	0.96
Medical research needs to be closely regulated in order to prevent harm to research participants	4.05	0.89
Participating in medical research is generally safe	3.51	1.03
If I volunteer for medical research, I know my personal information will be kept private and confidential	3.66	1.02
A lot of emphasis on medical research and scientific progress is likely to harm research volunteers	3.05	0.97

(continued)

Table 5.2: Mean responses for the Barriers and Facilitators to Research Participation Survey (continued)

Research Attitudes Questionnaire	Mean response (scale 1–5) 1 = Strongly disagree 5 = Strongly agree	SD
Medical research will find cures for many major diseases during my lifetime	3.59	0.97
Privacy concerns	Mean response (scale 1–6) 1 = Not worried at all 6 = Very worried	SD
Survey responses (n)	41	–
If you enrolled in research, tell us how worried you would be that someone not authorized would see your private information	3.27	2.20
If a research project collected your genetic information, how worried would you be that it might end up in a police database	3.56	2.28
Trust	Mean response (scale 1–5) 1 = Just about always 4 = Never	SD
Survey responses (n)	40	–
How much of the time do you think you can trust the government in Washington to do what is right?	3.25	0.81
Survey responses (n)	41	–
How much of the time do you think you can trust the Michigan State government to do what is right?	2.98	0.76
How much of the time do you think you can trust researchers at our university to do what is right?	2.44	0.63

Table 5.2: Mean responses for the Barriers and Facilitators to Research Participation Survey (continued)

Research Attitudes Questionnaire	Mean response (scale 1–5) 1 = Strongly disagree 5 = Strongly agree	SD
Financial wellness	Mean response (scale 1–4) 1 = Very well 4 = Not at all	SD
Survey responses (*n*)	38	–
With your current income, how well can you afford to meet your basic needs (housing, food, utilities, transportation, health care)?	2.34	0.94
Participation willingness	Mean response (scale 1–5) 1 = Not willing at all 5 = Willing	SD
Survey responses (*n*)	41	–
Willingness to participate in health research based on the following factors: the word 'genomics,' returning research results to participants, involving the entire family in the interview, venous blood specimen donation, blood spot donation, longitudinal research participation, and interviews completed in the respondent's home	3.34	1.59

experiences, and an additional 9.8 per cent reported that it was due to both race and gender (see Table 5.3). Thirteen (31.7 per cent) felt that their experiences of discrimination were due to 'other' reasons. When asked to specify, 23.1 per cent reported intelligence, 15.4 per cent reported no reason, and 23.1 per cent reported other reasons, including wealth (or lack thereof), age, and sexuality (see Table 5.3).

Table 5.3: Respondent rationale for perceived discrimination

Survey question	Frequency (%)
Main reason for perceived discrimination (*n*)	41
Race, ethnicity, ancestry, or national origin	14 (34.1)
Gender	1 (2.4)
Race and gender	4 (9.8)
Other	13 (31.7)
Race and other	3 (7.3)
Refused	6 (14.6)
If 'other' was selected, please specify why (*n*)	13
Intelligence	3 (23.1)
Wealth	1 (7.7)
Age	1 (7.7)
Sexuality	1 (7.7)
No reason	2 (15.4)
Incomprehensible	2 (15.4)
No response given	3 (23.1)

Discussion

This study aimed to determine whether hypothesized key factors affect genomic research participation among residents of Flint, Michigan. Most respondents disagreed with the notion that science does more harm than good, indicating that other factors hinder willingness to participate in research. Respondents indicated that some hesitation to participate was due to uncertainty of potential harms that may come from their involvement.

An unanticipated barrier to research participation was revealed – many respondents lacked an understanding of what research is and how it leads to advances in medical care and public health. Data collectors noted that many community members did not understand how public health research operates. Several respondents needed a description of research – that it starts with a researcher or team of researchers seeking an answer to a specific question. Some had difficulty conceiving what a researcher was. Some voiced that they had never connected getting approached to complete health surveys with discovering treatments or cures for diseases. If people do not know what research is and what it necessitates, they are likely to dismiss opportunities to engage in studies that aim to improve community health outcomes. This theme has been identified in similar studies, in which minority willingness to participate was negatively associated with a lack of understanding or awareness (Davis et al, 2019; Scherr et al, 2019). Our findings reaffirm the need to provide clear messaging to improve participation outcomes among minority populations.

Several study limitations merit attention. Our study population was predominantly composed of Black participants (78.1 per cent). This sample may not be representative of the population in Genesee county, which is reported to be 20.3 per cent Black (United States Census Bureau, 2019). Between 2015 and 2019, the Genesee county employment rate was 58.2 compared with the 22 per cent employment rate recorded in our sample (United States Census Bureau, 2019). However, our more Black and less employed sample helps us to understand some of the most marginalized people in the area.

Our results indicate that more deliberate communication is required regarding the purpose of public health interventions and medical research for informed decision making. Case studies across the nation support this. A study at one public US university sought to understand why students lost faith in university leadership during the COVID-19 pandemic (Osuna et al, 2021). They found that leadership did not 'engage in effective and timely communication with the specific goal of helping students to make informed decisions, especially regarding their finances'. On a national level, recent missteps by federal officials around COVID-19 communication have increased problems with mistrust, causing citizens to lose faith in the federal government (Weixel, 2022). Still, systematic review of studies around COVID-19 vaccination hesitancy based in mistrust is highest among Black women (Yasmin et al, 2021). The leader of a Black church congregation in Boston explained, 'Black people have been traumatized by a betrayal of the system forever for generations. And so the mistrust is about betrayal. People have believed in systems, and systems have failed them' (Simon, 2020).

Prior to COVID-19, the US had recently managed the 2014 Ebola epidemic, which revealed that communication around pandemic response was lacking (Madad and Spencer, 2021). However, in the context of COVID-19, this has not occurred. Instead, conflicting and politicized information has been shared and, in turn, people have developed a deep mistrust in science and life-saving public health measures (Madad and Spencer, 2021).

We offer this as an alternative framework. Instead of a pandemic response designed for the masses, future responses should immediately seek to detect barriers among marginalized sub-populations and directly address those barriers. In addition to educational campaigns, increasing public health awareness and understanding could be accomplished by utilizing popular news sources specific to each community, which could help reach specific audiences more readily, and promote public health participation.

References

Artiga, S., Kates, J., Michaud, J. and Hill, L. (2021) *Racial Diversity Within COVID-19 Vaccine Clinical Trials: Key Questions and Answers*, Kaiser Family Foundation. https://www.kff.org/racial-equity-and-health-policy/issue-brief/racial-diversity-within-covid-19-vaccine-clinical-trials-key-questions-and-answers/

Bodenheimer, T. and Grumbach, K. (2016) *Understanding Health Policy: A Clinical Approach*. http://accessmedicine.mhmedical.com/book.aspx?bookid=1790

Cuthbertson, C.A., Newkirk, C., Ilardo, J., Loveridge, S. and Skidmore, M. (2016) 'Angry, scared, and unsure: mental health consequences of contaminated water in Flint, Michigan', *Journal of Urban Health*, 93(6): 899–908. doi: 10.1007/s11524-016-0089-y

Davis, T.C., Arnold, C.L., Mills, G. and Miel, L. (2019) 'A qualitative study exploring barriers and facilitators of enrolling underrepresented populations in clinical trials and biobanking', *Frontiers in Cell and Developmental Biology*, 7(74). doi: 10.3389/fcell.2019.00074

De Vries, R.G., Tomlinson, T., Kim, H.M., Krenz, C., Haggerty, D., Ryan, K.A. and Kim, S.Y.H. (2016) 'Understanding the public's reservations about broad consent and study-by-study consent for donations to a biobank: results of a national survey', PLoS *One*, 11(7): e0159113. doi: 10.1371/journal.pone.0159113

Dembosky, A. (2021) 'No, the Tuskegee study is not the top reason some Black Americans question the COVID-19 vaccine', *KQED*, 25 February. www.kqed.org/news/11861810/no-the-tuske gee-study-is-not-the-top-reason-some-black-americans-quest ion-the-covid-19-vaccine

Durant, R.W., Wenzel, J.A., Scarinci, I.C., Paterniti, D.A., Fouad, M.N., Hurd, T.C. and Martin, M.Y. (2014) 'Perspectives on barriers and facilitators to minority recruitment for clinical trials among cancer center leaders, investigators, research staff, and referring clinicians: Enhancing Minority Participation in Clinical Trials (EMPaCT)', *Cancer*, 120: 1097–105. doi: 10.1002/cncr.28574

Ekezie, W., Czyznikowska, B.M., Rohit, S., Harrison, J., Miah, N., Campbell-Morris, P. and Khunti, K. (2021) 'The views of ethnic minority and vulnerable communities towards participation in COVID-19 vaccine trials', *Journal of Public Health*, 43(2): e258–e260. doi: 10.1093/pubmed/fdaa196

Fisher, E.R., Pratt, R., Esch, R., Kocher, M., Wilson, K., Lee, W. and Zierhut, H.A. (2020) 'The role of race and ethnicity in views toward and participation in genetic studies and precision medicine research in the United States: a systematic review of qualitative and quantitative studies', *Molecular Genetics & Genomic Medicine*, 8(2): e1099. doi: 10.1002/mgg3.1099

Fortenberry, G.Z., Reynolds, P., Burrer, S.L., Johnson-Lawrence, V., Wang, A., Schnall, A., Pullins, P., Kieszak, S., Bayleyegn, T. and Wolkin, A. (2018) 'Assessment of behavioral health concerns in the community affected by the Flint Water Crisis – Michigan (USA) 2016', *Prehospital and Disaster Medicine*, 33(3): 256–65. doi: 10.1017/S1049023X18000250

Jaklevic, M.C. (2020) 'Researchers strive to recruit hard-hit minorities into COVID-19 vaccine trials', *JAMA*, 324(9): 826–28. doi: 10.1001/jama.2020.11244

Katz, R.V., Kegeles, S.S., Kressin, N.R., Green, B.L., Wang, M.Q., James, S.A., Russell, S.L. and Claudio, C. (2006) 'The Tuskegee Legacy Project: willingness of minorities to participate in biomedical research', *Journal of Health Care for the Poor and Underserved*, 17(4): 698–715. doi: 10.1353/hpu.2006.0126

Madad, S. and Spencer, C. (2021) 'The USA's response to the 2014 Ebola outbreak could have informed its COVID-19 response', *The Lancet*, 397(10278): 965–6. doi: 10.1016/S0140-6736(21)00433-5

McDonald, J.A., Vadaparampil, S., Bowen, D., Magwood, G., Obeid, J.S., Jefferson, M., Drake, R., Gebregziabher, M. and Halbert, C.H. (2014) 'Intentions to donate to a biobank in a national sample of African Americans', *Public Health Genomics*, 17(3): 173–82. doi: 10.1159/000360472

McQuillan, G.M., Porter, K.S., Agelli, M. and Kington, R. (2003) 'Consent for genetic research in a general population: the NHANES experience', *Genetics in Medicine*, 5(1): 35–42. doi: 10.1097/00125817-200301000-00006

McQuillan, G.M., Pan, Q. and Porter, K.S. (2006) 'Consent for genetic research in a general population: an update on the National Health and Nutrition Examination Survey experience', *Genetics in Medicine*, 8(6): 354–60. doi: 10.1097/01.gim.0000223552.70393.08

Momplaisir, F., Haynes, N., Nkwihoreze, H., Nelson, M., Werner, R.M. and Jemmott, J. (2021) 'Understanding drivers of coronavirus disease 2019 vaccine hesitancy among Blacks', *Clinical Infectious Diseases*, 73(10): 1784–9. doi: 10.1093/cid/ciab102

Nguyen, K.H., Srivastav, A., Razzaghi, H., Williams, W., Lindley, M.C., Jorgensen, C., Abad, N. and Singleton, J.A. (2021) 'COVID-19 vaccination intent, perceptions, and reasons for not vaccinating among groups prioritized for early vaccination – United States, September and December 2020', *MMWR* and *Morbidity and Mortality Weekly Report*, 70(6): 217–22. doi: 10.15585/mmwr.mm7006e3

Osuna, A.I., Darcy, K., Woessner, Z.W. and Hamm, J.A. (2021) *Perceived Student Vulnerabilities During the COVID-19 Pandemic*, TRUSST Lab. http://trusstlab.com/resources

Rubright, J.D., Cary, M.S., Karlawish, J.H. and Kim, S.Y. (2011) 'Measuring how people view biomedical research: reliability and validity analysis of the Research Attitudes Questionnaire', *Journal of Empirical Research on Human Research Ethics*, 6(1): 63–8. doi: 10.1525/jer.2011.6.1.63

Scherr, C.L., Ramesh, S., Marshall-Fricker, C. and Perera, M.A. (2019) 'A review of African Americans' beliefs and attitudes about genomic studies: opportunities for message design', *Frontiers in Genetics*, 10(1): 548. doi: 10.3389/fgene.2019.00548

Simon, S. (2020) 'Fighting COVID-19 vaccine mistrust in the Black community', NPR, 19 December. www.npr.org/transcripts/948316306

Sneed, R.S., Key, K., Bailey, S. and Johnson-Lawrence, V. (2020) 'Social and psychological consequences of the COVID-19 pandemic in African-American communities: lessons from Michigan', *Psychological Trauma: Theory, Research, Practice, and Policy*, 12(5): 446–8. doi: 10.1037/tra0000881

United States Census Bureau (2019) 'Quick Facts: Genesee County, Michigan'. www.census.gov/quickfacts/geneseecountymichigan

Weixel, N. (2022) 'CDC leader faces precarious political moment', The Hill, 1 October. https://thehill.com/policy/healthcare/589097-cdc-leader-faces-precarious-political-moment

Yasmin, F., Najeeb, H., Moeed, A., Naeem, U., Asghar, M.S., Chughtai, N.U., Yousaf, Z., Seboka, B.T., Ullah, I., Lin, C.Y. and Pakpour, A.H. (2021) 'COVID-19 vaccine hesitancy in the United States: a systematic review', *Frontiers in Public Health*, 9. doi: 10.3389/fpubh.2021.770985

PART II

The Violence of Under/ De-Development

SIX

Gaza: The Right to Life or the Right to Health During COVID-19

Ayman Qwaider

Introduction

"I have no trust in the collapsing healthcare system in Gaza, and it would be impossible to combat the virus if it hits us here. Finally, the Israeli blockade has protected us from the virus." This was a segment of a rather hopeful conversation I had with my father back in May 2020 when the frequent border closure resulted in no-community-transmitted COVID-19 cases in Gaza. However, three months later, the outbreak of the virus in Gaza was imminent, and the pandemic's tragic implications on a place with one of the most dense refugee populations in the world were inevitable. This meant that preventive measures such as ensuring social distancing and self-quarantine were impossible in a place with an estimated population of 5,800 people per square kilometre (UNRWA, 2012). Gaza's dense population, however, was not the only factor influencing an effective response to the outbreak. The coastal enclaved Gaza Strip had been particularly vulnerable prior to the onset of the COVID-19 pandemic, as Gaza suffers from a prolonged de-development process (Roy, 2016) due to years of Israeli blockade and successive wars which have devastated Gaza's economy, education, health, and livelihood. The imposition of the blockade on Gaza, described by the UN as an 'open-air prison' (Al Jazeera, 2010), and the limited movement of goods have led to troubling shortages of medicine and other medical supplies, including ventilators. In this chapter, I offer a brief review of Gaza's pre-pandemic health sector and explore the barriers to providing an adequate response to the pandemic. I then move to explain some of the practices implemented to living and responding to the COVID-19 pandemic under such obstacles. I highlight some of the socio-political and health implications of the pandemic on Gaza's vulnerable population. Considering Israeli military aggression against Gaza in May 2021, I argue that an analysis of the medical and health response to a global pandemic should address the context of a systematic de-development process in the Gaza Strip which increased the Strip's vulnerability to the outbreak.

Surviving the unliveable: the pre-COVID-19 Gaza disaster

A UN report released in 2012 warned that Gaza would be unliveable in 2020 (UNRWA, 2012). The report anticipated that between 2012 and 2020 there would be a 500,000 person increase in the population of the Gaza Strip, and recommended that such demographic growth demanded a similar development of essential infrastructure to ensure the provision of certain services including, electricity, water, health and education. However, instead of the proposed long-term economic growth, Gaza continued to endure more years of a stifling political siege, which continued to inflict more devastating impact on every aspect of life. In this section, I briefly explain the pre-COVID-19 context of the Gaza Strip. I stress that improving the overall life aspects of Palestinian people will only be possible when the root cause and the structural violence Palestinians endure daily have been adequately addressed. I argue that an adequate and effective response to the COVID-19 pandemic is inextricably bound to understanding and addressing the political context. I explain how Gaza's increased risk of vulnerability because of the pandemic, a concern expressed by major human rights organizations, is rooted in a historical reality in which Palestinians have experienced multilayers of structural political violence. Years of policies of institutionalized oppression and structural violence have forced the population in Gaza into extreme poverty and high unemployment, and impoverished the health and education sectors (Roy, 2016). Therefore, as Yara Asi (2020) explains, 'no analysis of the fragmented Palestinian health sector today is complete without an understanding of the factors that have brought it to its current state' and both 'social and political determinants of health are deeply embedded in the ways the occupation and its restrictions manifest in all aspects of Palestinian daily life'.

How did the siege affect the health sector?

The Gaza Strip is a coastal piece of land of no more than 365 square kilometres. It is home to more than 2 million people, 1.4 million of whom are refugees (Human Rights Council, 2019). Refugees thus constitute the demographic majority of the Strip: they were made refugees when forcibly depopulated from their homes and villages when the state of Israel was established in 1948 and during the 1967 war. In 2007, the Israeli government imposed a political blockade over the Gaza Strip, which is considered by mainstream human rights organizations as a state-sponsored collective punishment policy (ICRC, 2010). The Israeli air-land-sea blockade over the enclaved Gaza Strip has exposed a large number of the population to more unemployment and uncertainty, and made them highly dependent on international aid. The blockade has had devastating impacts on health, jobs, food security, education, clean water availability and power supplies. As a result of the siege, the health sector in Gaza witnessed an ongoing state of emergency even before the first COVID-19 case was reported, and alarming concerns and fears among both population and authorities about the ability of a fragile health system to cope with the COVID-19 outbreak.

For example, one of the most important public health recommendations from the World Health Organization in face of the pandemic has been ensuring personal hygiene and sanitation. However, the siege has had grave impact on the water infrastructure in Gaza. Gaza suffers from the lack of clean drinkable water with only 4 per cent of its freshwater being drinkable (B'Tselem, 2014). In 2005, Israel bombed the main power plant in Gaza causing damage and affecting the power supply to the Strip. Shortage of electricity constrained the environmental management and treatment of sewage water. An estimate of 108,000 cubic metres of untreated sewage was pumped into the Mediterranean Sea, polluting its water as well as polluting 97 per cent of the aquifers' water (McAuley and Balousha, 2019). This also meant that Gaza is particularly vulnerable to the spread of diseases (Shira Efron et al, 2018, 32). Besides, the siege has had its toll on essential health infrastructure and facilities. In the Occupied Palestinian Territories, Israeli occupation controls all imports and exports, banning or restricting materials perceived as 'dual use'. This ban is even stricter in the Strip, and materials banned include, for example, cement for building health care facilities, generators, certain medications or medical equipment, and fuel, essential for the power supply in Gaza due to the electricity crisis (Barhoum, 2018).

Since 2008, Gaza has faced successive brutal military aggressions that have severely damaged some essential health care infrastructures and facilities. The challenge to rebuild or reconstruct such infrastructure becomes even higher due to the import restrictions and the blockade. In 2014, for example, Israel destroyed thousands of homes and an estimated 73 medical facilities, most of which were not rebuilt. These regular assaults have also resulted in the deaths of medical staff, and a shortage of medical personnel (OCHA, 2015). The closure of Gaza borders has also had a negative impact on the capacity building of local medical and healthcare personnel living in Gaza. It is immensely difficult to access specialized health trainings needed to develop staff skills and provide quality care to Palestinian patients. Consequently, this has negatively impacted public and community health development (WHO, 2019).

The Israeli blockade has also led to a severe shortage of drugs and medical supplies such as medications, spare parts for machinery and disposable items. At the onset of the pandemic, Gaza also suffered from the lack of coronavirus testing kits. In April 2021, statistics from Ministry of Health in Gaza showed there was 'a serious shortage of 45 per cent of the essential drugs list, and 31 per cent of medical consumables, and 65 per cent of laboratory products and blood banking supplies' (PCHR, 2020). The Ministry of Health also announced it was lacking in hospital beds, intensive care units, ventilators and protective gear (PCHR, 2020). In fact, as the pandemic hit globally, reports indicated the hospitals' lack of readiness to deal with a surge in COVID-19 cases. According to Physicians for Human Rights (2020), there were only 70 available intensive care beds across the Palestinian Territories with only 45 operational ventilators for more than 2 million residents, the majority of whom are refugee women and children.

Gaza's electricity crisis has also severely impacted the health sector. The frequent shortage of fuel as a result of banning the entry of fuel needed to operate the power plant puts further pressure on health facilities, and has led in many instances to failure in providing proper medical care. Power cuts ranging between 16 and 20 hours a day put extreme pressure on medical facilities, leading to excessive dependence on generators, which also need the fuel that is not available due to the blockade.

This extreme state of the health sector has led the Palestinian Authority (PA) to outsource its patients to hospitals in the West Bank and Israel. Palestinian patients are often referred to hospitals in the West Bank and in Israel for medical treatment, especially given the lack of certain tests, scans, treatment or expertise due to the siege. Patients from Gaza, with medical referrals, still have to apply for military permits to be hospitalized in the West Bank or Israel. In December 2019, however, WHO reported that only 64 per cent of medical permits were approved from Gaza. This access fluctuated according to border closures and political tensions. For example, in Spring 2020 and after the PA's threat to stop civil coordination with Israel in response to the latter's annexation plan, reports show a decrease in urgent medical permits approval, with rates reaching 50 per cent. This led to denying access to ventilators and adequate medical response to COVID-19 cases from Gaza.

Managing the pandemic during a time of crisis

With only two entry and exit points into the Gaza Strip, my father's hopeful remark seemed to hold its ground; the blockade and its implication over the restriction of movements continued to be seen as beneficial as it reduced the potential of an outbreak. Travellers returning home to Gaza from abroad were subjected to quarantine in designated facilities. The management of the pandemic seemed illusively possible. These hopeful remarks did not last for long, however, for on 24 August 2020, the first case of coronavirus was reported in Gaza, and the concern for the vulnerable population became a reality that urgently required fast intervention and measures put in place to prevent a disastrous outbreak. But what do these preventive measures mean for Palestinians living in Gaza, and were measures such as lockdowns effective in managing the spread of the pandemic?

In this section, I explain the measures taken to control the spread of the pandemic and the major ways in which the pandemic increased people's social, economic and health vulnerability.

Once the first cases of COVID-19 were reported outside the quarantine facilities, the authorities in Gaza tried to follow the global health protocols to maintain public health and safety. Initial measures included imposing 48-hour curfews across the Gaza Strip, and suspending work in public and private sectors, closing educational institutions including schools and universities, open markets, wedding halls and clubs, and banning all gatherings including mosque prayers and church masses, in an attempt to contain the virus, and to contact-trace individuals who contracted the virus. The efforts, thus, focused on complete closures of schools, public markets, social gatherings, and the Gaza beach, which is the main recreational destination for the people of Gaza. Safety measures including social distancing, maintaining personal hygiene, and wearing masks were also imposed. These measures were partially effective, yet a complete lockdown for longer periods of time did not seem feasible given the dependence on everyday incomes for survival. Such measures fluctuated between easing, increasing, or being lifted according to the surge or the lowering of active cases that were reported between August 2020 and April 2021. For example, as cases were surging in the month of April, the authorities introduced a ban on vehicle movement on the weekend, and from sunset on weekdays, and introduced stronger legal measures and fines against people violating home quarantine or compulsory quarantine in Khan Younis. Police forces were deployed to ensure curfews were respected, and sand berms were erected to isolate refugee camps and crowded neighbourhoods with high infection rates (Estrin, 2021).

These measures were unstable and largely linked to the insecurity of the economic situation in Gaza, where levels of unemployment reached a high of 45 per cent – and of poverty of 53 per cent – and people were thus much more dependent on international aid (Gisha, 2020) due to extended years of blockade and political instabilities. Families depend on casual day-to-day income to secure food and basic daily needs. Over the years, many families have become dependent mainly on humanitarian aid parcels as well as daily individual jobs to gain some livelihood to secure limited income for their family members. Lockdowns, which led to suspending daily jobs, have negatively impacted many young people by preventing them from putting food on the family table by the end of the day. With the absence of welfare support provided by the government, these measures put massive pressure on insecure individuals, demanding from them the ethical responsibility of abiding by lockdown rules to minimize the impact of the virus, yet such individual responsibility meant they risked not meeting their basic needs. For example, lockdowns introduced affecting vehicle movement meant taxi drivers who are dependent on their daily income lost that income and became more vulnerable. Authorities have also demanded people stay at home if they feel unwell, again putting the pressure on individuals to make the right ethical choices, yet a lot of people lied about having symptoms or hid their illness to engage in their daily business in order to secure their family's daily income.

Social distancing and isolating communities are measures taken by many countries around the world that were foreign to the extremely-crowded refugee camps in Gaza. For example, the idea of social distancing was impossible to fully implement given the density of the population, especially in refugee camps. Besides, social interaction and solidarity have been essential for the people of Gaza in the face of the political Israeli blockade, international isolation, and regular military aggressions, amid other adversaries. I recall that, when the Israeli Military Occupation Forces used to conduct ground incursions in my refugee camp of Nuseirat, in the middle of the Gaza Strip, my whole extended family would come together to support each other through the military operation. People are interdependent on each other to survive the cruelty of the siege and aggressions, and this social factor has been one of the very few coping mechanisms and means to fostering resilience that Palestinians in Gaza had.

Some of the measures taken by the local authorities also created a sense of social stigma. For example, to ensure people who contracted COVID-19 abide by quarantine, the authorities initially employed police forces to patrol the homes of those in quarantine to ensure that neither patients nor their families present in the same house went into the community. Besides the social stigma, the presence of police forces also risked people's access to food and basic needs, which meant people did not get tested even if they had symptoms in order to avoid such situations; this also meant that whatever numbers the Ministry of Health could report with its limited access to testing kits were non-representative of the actual numbers of COVID-19 cases in Gaza.

These are some of the measures authorities in Gaza took in the battle against the pandemic with very little resources. The increase of community transmission meant containing the virus was no longer possible, especially with the inability to impose stricter measures. For example, WHO reported that in April 2021 alone, there were around 35,882 new COVID-19 cases, with the number of active cases surging by 58 per cent. In that month, 288 people died of COVID-19, bringing the overall fatality toll to 899. In the last week of the month, an average of 2,500 tests were conducted daily, with a positivity rate of 30 per cent. In April, Gaza was declared a red zone, portraying the extreme level of community transmitted cases. WHO's assessment report on 22 April stated that 'infections in the Gaza Strip account for two-thirds of all cases in the [occupied Palestinian territory] oPt, with some signs of reaching a plateau but the situation remains critical' according to WHO (2021).

This spike in COVID-19 cases in late April had a tormenting impact on a health system that was already struggling before the pandemic. The pandemic magnified the shortages of medical supplies and equipment in the Gaza Strip caused by the siege, yet this global health crisis did not lead to alleviating any of the restrictions imposed on importing medical supplies. Asi (2020) explains that

even after the onset of the pandemic, medical equipment suppliers who had worked directly with the Palestinian

Ministry of Health to import goods were having trouble getting approval from Israel's Coordinator of Government Activities in the Territories (COGAT). One had been trying to get medical equipment into Gaza, unsuccessfully, for three years.

Gaza also continued to suffer insufficient access to ventilators, with only three ventilators per 100,000 people. Besides the shortage in testing kits, the ongoing power outages threatened the accuracy of COVID-19 testing, as some testing kits, requiring to be kept in a certain temperature to prevent false negative results, were damaged due to electricity cuts.

The pandemic has also highlighted the disparity of the context in Palestine and Israel, and the political implications of managing a pandemic while under military and political occupation. For example, not only has Israel refused to lift any of its restrictions on the Gaza Strip, but it increased the level of permit refusal for patients needing urgent medical treatment in hospitals in the West Bank and Israel. That disparity can be clearly seen through the vaccine roll out. While Israel prides itself to being one of the first countries to have the majority of its population vaccinated, up until April 2021, only 3 per cent of Palestinians living in the Occupied Palestinian Territories had received a first dose (OCHA 2021). Under International law, Israel as the occupying power is responsible for public health in Gaza and the West Bank, yet Israel denies that responsibility. Israel also attempted to provide conditional medical relief to Gaza by tying this to political gains, such as Defense Minister Naftali's remarks that any relief given to Gaza would be on the condition of the release of two Israeli soldiers lost in the 2014 aggression on Gaza. But most importantly, Israel's colonial activities did not cease during the pandemic. Before May 2021, Palestinians in the neighbourhoods of Sheikh Jarrah and Silwan were being threatened with displacement from their homes by Israeli settlers. Palestinian neighbourhoods in East Jerusalem, like all Occupied East Jerusalem, have been under Israeli military occupation since 1967. But on Sunday 2 May, an Israeli court ruled in favour of Israeli settlers' eviction of Palestinian families living in Sheikh Jarrah and taking ownership of their homes, an example of Israeli state-sanctioned ethnic cleansing. These evictions are part of a wider Israeli push to change the demographics of Jerusalem by removing Palestinians and replacing them with Israeli Jewish settlers. For months, Palestinian peaceful protesters in Sheikh Jarrah were met with violence; Israel also continued to block all entrances to the Sheikh Jarrah neighbourhood to restrict media coverage of the peaceful protests.

In fact, tension has been building for months across Palestinian Territories including in the isolated Gaza. The situation in Sheikh Jarrah is significant for the Palestinians because it is a manifestation of the ongoing Israeli colonial project. As NBCNEWS (2021) reports, 'The expansion of Jewish settlements in Sheikh Jarrah, which is on land that helps form the final link in a settlement circle surrounding East Jerusalem – an area that Palestinians hope will be the capital of a future state.' In order to distract attention from the events of Sheikh Jarrah, Israel has continued its policies of inflicting more punishment and humiliation on Palestinians in the West Bank and Gaza.

Shifting priorities: the right to life or the right to health

While the impact of a global pandemic has not alleviated the structural violence that Palestinians experience daily because of the Israeli occupation, Palestinians in Gaza had to endure further risk to their lives and livelihoods as a result of the Israeli aggression in May 2021. During a time when Gaza's health sector was already struggling to cope with managing a global pandemic, hospitals in Gaza had to deal with the implications of a military aggression. COVID-19 was no longer my father's major concern, as the responsibility to provide safety for his family during the heavy bombing was much more urgent.

With no bomb shelters to seek refuge in, Palestinians in the Gaza Strip were facing the loss of their homes, as residential buildings were being razed to the ground, sometimes with their residents sleeping in them.

The medical advice to stay at home to protect against the spread of the virus was completely irrelevant in a context where thousands of families sought refuge in UNRWA (United Nations Relief and Works Agency for Palestine Refugees in the Near East) schools. Forty-one thousand Palestinians were displaced into UNRWA schools, crowded into classrooms, both experiencing a recurrent trauma that they have been through in 2014, 2012, and 2008, and the risk of a wider COVID-19 transmission. Moreover, Israel attacked and destroyed the only COVID-19 testing clinic in the Gaza Strip, which prevented people's access to COVID-19 testing during and in the aftermath of the aggression. Statistics for COVID-19 cases in Gaza were not available for some time after the aggression. In many ways, the attack intensified the severity of the risk of the pandemic for the people of Gaza, whose right to life was being attacked. Precautionary or preventive measures to prevent the spread of the virus such as wearing masks or ensuring social distancing were people's last concerns when they were asked to evacuate their houses before they were bombed. Photos showing some people evacuating their homes with their masks on were a stark reminder that amid this dispossession, the threat of COVID-19 was still there. In fact, the severe attack was a glaring example of the disparity of access to health for the people living under occupation, and the importance of contextualizing a health response that considers the political and the historical reality of the people, as well as the demand for a just resolution to the root cause for such disparity.

The COVID-19 crisis in Gaza continues to be an alarming concern. It has revealed the troubling level of vulnerability of the 2 million Palestinians living in Gaza. Consecutive Israeli governments have presented Gaza as a separate geographical and political entry as it is under the control of Gaza since 2007, and to disconnect the Gaza Palestinians from the wider Palestinian community. The limitations of responding to the deadly pandemic in Gaza remains under the responsibility of Israel as an occupying power and control. This is an urgent time, more than ever before, for the international community to hold Israel accountable for the wellbeing of the Palestinian people in Gaza.

References

Al Jazeera (2010) 'UN Envoy: Gaza an open-air prison', *Al Jazeera*, 2 March. www.aljazeera.com/news/2010/3/2/un-envoy-gaza-an-open-air-prison

Asi, Y. (2020) 'Occupation in the time of Covid-19: holding Israel accountable for Palestinian health', *AlShabaka*. 12 March. www.juancole.com/2020/12/occupation-accountable-palestinian.html

Barhoum, L. (2018) 'Israel tightens Gaza blockade, civilians bear the brunt', a brief by the Norwegian Refugee Council, *Oxfam and Premiere Urgence Internationale*, July. www.nrc.no/globalassets/pdf/briefing-notes/mb-gaza-israel-blockade-civilians-270818-en.pdf

B'Tselem (2014) 'Over 90% of water in Gaza Strip unfit for drinking', 9 February. www.btselem.org/gaza_strip/20140209_gaza_water_crisis

Estrin, D. (2021) 'In Gaza, pandemic forces tough choices and health care system hangs by a thread', *NPR*, 4 February. www.npr.org/2021/02/04/963251171/in-gaza-pandemic-forces-tough-choices-and-health-care-system-hangs-by-a-thread

Gisha (2020) 'Gaza unemployment rate in the second quarter of 2020: 49.1%', 21 September. https://gisha.org/en/gaza-unemployment-rate-in-the-second-quarter-of-2020-49-1/

Human Rights Council (2019) 'Report of the detailed findings of the independent international Commission of inquiry on the protests in the Occupied Palestinian Territory', Fortieth Session, 18 March. www.ohchr.org/sites/default/files/HRBodies/HRC/RegularSessions/Session40/Documents/A_HRC_40_74_CRP2.pdf

ICRC (2010) 'Gaza closure: not another year!' Press release, 14 June. www.icrc.org/en/doc/resources/documents/update/palestine-update-140610.htm

McAuley, J. and Balousha, H. (2019) 'A summer day at the beach? For many Gazans, the conflict has put an end to that, too', *Washington Post*, 28 August. www.washingtonpost.com/world/a-summer-day-at-the-beach-for-many-gazans-the-conflict-has-put-an-end-to-that-too/2019/08/28/fee73450-c4e9-11e9-8bf7-cde2d9e09055_story.html

NBCNEWS (2021) 'Biden followed pro-Israel U.S. precedent. But new critics shake the status quo', 14 May. www.nbcnews.com/news/world/far-away-tense-jerusalem-squad-pressures-biden-israel-palestinian-conflict-n1267275

OCHA (2015) 'Key figures on the hostilities', 23 June. www.ochaopt.org/content/key-figures-2014-hostilities

OCHA (2021) 'COVID-19 emergency situation report 30 April 2021', 6 May. www.ochaopt.org/content/covid-19-emergency-situation-report-30-april-2021

Palestinian Centre for Human Rights (PCHR) (2020) 'Gaza Strip on verge of real collapse due to coronavirus outbreak and ongoing Israeli closure', 28 August. https://pchrgaza.org/en/gaza-strip-on-verge-of-real-collapse-due-to-coronavirus-outbreak-and-ongoing-israeli-closure/

Physicians for Human Rights (2020) 'Corona in the Gaza Strip – only 70 ICU beds available', 25 March. www.phr.org.il/en/corona-in-the-gaza-strip-only-70-icu-beds-available/

Roy, S. (2016) *The Gaza Strip: The Political Economy of De-development*. 3rd ed. Institute for Palestine Studies.

Shira Efron S., Fischbach J.R., Blum I., Karimov R.I., Moore M. and RAND Corporation (2018) 'The public health impacts of Gaza's water crisis: Analysis and policy options'.

UNRWA (2012) *Gaza in 2020: A Liveable Place?*, 28 August. www.unrwa.org/newsroom/press-releases/gaza-2020-liveable-place

WHO (2019) *Right to Health in the Occupied Palestinian Territory: 2018.* WHO Regional Office for the Eastern Mediterranean. https://reliefweb.int/report/occupied-palestinian-territory/who-right-health-occupied-palestinian-territory-2018

World Health Organization, Occupied Palestinian Territories (2019) *Health Access Barriers for Patients in the Occupied Palestinian Territory,* December. www.emro.who.int/images/stories/palestine/documents/Dec_2019_Monthly_Updated.pdf?ua=1

SEVEN

'You Are No More Required': COVID-19 Unmasks False Development Policies

Farida Akhter

Introduction

Many ready-made garment (RMG) workers in Bangladesh, the daughters and sons of small scale farmers, have been thrown out of their jobs since the COVID-19 pandemic started. The owners of the factories have declared 'You are no more required'; but were they welcome back in their village homes? No, that was not the case either. They were not required in the farming households where they belonged before. Now their families would be happier if they could return to their jobs in the cities. This research highlights the effects of the preventive and mitigating measures against the COVID-19 pandemic on the people in two major sectors: small scale farmers and RMG workers. These people have suffered the most since the first COVID-19 cases in the country in March 2020.

Virus versus neoliberal development policies

Since its independence, Bangladesh has followed the development path mostly dictated by the international and multilateral agencies such as the World Bank, IMF and various private foundations such as Ford and Rockefeller Foundations. In the 1980s, it adopted the neoliberal development paradigm, where the market dictates vital national concerns such as health, food, nutrition, livelihood and human behaviour. Systematic downplaying of vital national concerns and the strategy to dismantle or reconfigure existing socioeconomic relations and institutions contributed to the collapse of public health (Khan and Rahman, 2019). The onset of the COVID-19 pandemic made this collapse instantly visible, signalling the precarious and vulnerable conditions of all other sectors (UBINIG, 2020d). Modern development policy assumes that the more food production is industrialized, the more agriculture will release 'surplus labour'. These labourers, free from farming, will gradually migrate to the industrialized urban centres looking for jobs with higher pay. Consequently, small household farming will wither away and large-scale industrial production units will emerge (UBINIG, 2020c).

During the pandemic, thousands of RMG workers and other informal sector workers, small businesses and private offices lost work and returned to their villages. The rural economy was not able to integrate those additional workers. Their skills did not match with farming.

The novel coronavirus with newer impacts

The novel coronavirus, COVID-19, highlighted the complete unpreparedness of the government, of health care facilities and of preventive public health measures. The crisis triggered by the COVID-19 pandemic spilt over to economic, social, cultural and political spheres. The socioeconomic challenges were obvious; the difficulty of keeping daily lives functioning with the minimal disruption to livelihoods, particularly of the poor and vulnerable was vividly apparent. The cultural crisis was manifested in stigmatizing those who were infected with the virus. Orders to force people to 'stay at home' did not work, when livelihood questions were uncertain (UBINIG, 2020c).

On 26 March 2020, the government announced a 'public holiday' of ten days, which was then extended until May 2020 to control the outbreak. By 15 December 2020, the number of COVID-19 positive cases was 494,209 and there had been 7,129 deaths according to the daily bulletins of the Directorate General of Health Services under the Ministry of Health & Family Welfare.

UBINIG reports on health and agriculture during April and May 2020 (2020a, 2020b) showed the disastrous consequences of the neoliberal development policy that had systematically undermined and dismantled the social and collective responsibilities of the state towards its members. In the present global order, Bangladesh has hardly any independent capacity to protect its citizens but is increasing configured as a means of global capital accumulation.

The situation of agriculture and the farmers in the pandemic

The agriculture sector is comprised of millions of small scale farmers owning less than 1 hectare of land – these make up 80 per cent of farming households, with 14 per cent of these being medium farms and 9 per cent large farms (Government of Bangladesh, 2015). Agriculture is still the largest singular employment generating sector in Bangladesh, accounting for over 40 per cent of employment.

Modern agriculture requiring cash investment on the package of fertilizers, irrigation, pesticides and high yielding variety (HYV) seeds led to farmers' indebtedness as prices rose due to the withdrawal of subsidies and increased commercialization. Returns declined due to high overhead costs and low prices at the market. The policy towards industrialization led to the outflow of the young rural population to urban areas in search of jobs in the RMG, large informal and service sectors. Agriculture was left with the older generation who needed to keep the land in cultivation. Climate change, natural disasters and the price uncertainties of agricultural products have made agriculture less lucrative than other sectors. Many small scale farmers sold land to pay for the travel costs of sending their sons to the Middle East to earn income.

The government programme on educating girls coupled with reduced agriculture income prompted farmers to send their daughters to the RMG factories in the cities and their sons to the Middle East to earn income. The global pandemic has affected jobs overseas. The farmers felt the brunt with sons returning from the Middle East, Italy and Malaysia.

Farmers were already facing hardships. A 2020 UBINIG survey across 17 villages in three districts showed that 97 per cent of farmers faced high food prices, 66 per cent had reduced food consumption, 49 per cent cut the number of meals per day and 66 per cent decreased consumption of fresh vegetables and fruits. Maintaining farming operations became harder: 85 per cent of farmers had difficulty getting seeds and other agricultural inputs, and 87 per cent had trouble recruiting labourers. Selling agricultural produce was harder for 97 per cent of farmers, the income from other non-farm sources was reduced for 94 per cent of farmers, and the ability to find off-farm work was impossible for 100 per cent of farmers (UBINIG, 2020e).

Farmers were directly affected by the lockdown. According to UBINIG (2020b), the farming community, particularly small scale farmers who had many of their winter crops in the field, could not market vegetables and rice due to the lack of available transport. The lockdown severely affected over 8.4 million day agricultural labourers. Migrant agricultural labourers during the paddy crop planting and harvesting season were not able to move and hence were without work. On the other hand, medium-sized farms also suffered a lack of labourers for the rice harvest. A government subsidy of Tk2 billion had been focused on the mechanization of harvesting, thus depriving small farmers and agricultural labourers of their livelihood. Environmentalists and agro-ecologists are concerned that mechanization will further displace agricultural labourers (UNIBIG, 2020b).

RMG sector and the workers in the COVID-19 pandemic

The RMG sector earns US$34 billion per year and accounts for 84 per cent of Bangladesh's exports. Export-oriented industrialization policy was particularly encouraged given the low capital investment, availability of cheap labour and quick returns. The empowerment of women was later seen as an impact of the industry.

More than 4,600 small and large RMG factories contribute to 36 per cent of manufacturing employment, engaging 4.1 million workers, mostly young women. According to Bangladesh's Labour Force Survey in 2016, 71.5 per cent of women and 59.6 of men working in the RMG sector were 29 years old or younger. International Aid Agencies like Asian Development Bank (ADB) labelled the workers as 'industrious, disciplined and low-cost women workers' (ADB, 2020). These workers start with a monthly minimum wage of Tk8,000 (US$95) – one of the lowest wages in the global garments supply chain – with overtime making the working day over 12 hours long. According to an International Labour Organization (ILO) study, only two-third (64 per cent) of the workers reported that their employers follow the legal limit of overtime work (ILO, 2017). The workers are working more than 14 hours and often have two shifts of night duties from 6 pm to 6 am. These low-paid workers were interested in overtime work, as it increased their total monthly income to between Tk10,000 (US$118) and Tk14,000 (US$165).

On 25 March 2020, the government announced a stimulus package of Tk5000 crore (US$58.7 million) for the export-oriented sector. Factory owners were asked to pay the wages and salaries of workers and employees, but they did not pay full wages for March and April 2020. They did not pay outstanding wages. The workers complained that RMG workers brought billions of dollars to the factory owners every year, yet the factory owners did not stand beside them during this critical crisis period. Many workers complained that they were not paid for the previous two months or more.

The precarious situation of the RMG workers was not due to coronavirus alone. The RMG workers were not being paid regularly, most workers had three to five months of pay overdue and were already living in very difficult situations. In 2019, a Bangladesh Institute of Labour Studies study found that 56 per cent of RMG workers procured their essential commodities on credit, and 72 per cent could not get proper medical treatment due to low wages, while the pandemic amplified their crises even more (*Dhaka Tribune*, 2020b).

A Global Alliance for Improved Nutrition (GAIN) study showed that 43 per cent of workers in the RMG industry suffer from malnutrition. About 7.9 per cent of Bangladesh's GDP is lost annually due to anaemia among the workers (*Dhaka Tribune*, 2020c).

Another survey, conducted by Clear Vision Workplace (CVW) showed that 35 per cent to 40 per cent of RMG workers needed eyeglasses for better vision. Participants in the survey of 18,000 apparel workers in 2018–19 received eyeglasses under the CVW programme (*Dhaka Tribune*, 2020a).

The most striking information about the RMG sector was that the ratio of female to male garment workers was falling. The ready-made garment sector was known for the high ratio of young female workers. In the 1980s and 1990s, according to the ILO report, 90 per cent of RMG workers were women. But this proportion is gradually declining. A recent ILO study found the proportion of women workers in surveyed RMG enterprises declined from 63.4 per cent of the workforce in 2010 to 61.17 per cent in 2018 (cited in New Age, 2020).

According to the Centre for Policy Dialogue (CPD), the changing female-male ratio was due to automation. The sweater and knit composite segment has more male workers

(60.5 per cent) than female workers due to the nature of work and automation (cited in New Age, 2020).

The Bangladesh Garment Manufacturers and Exporters Association and its dealings with RMG workers

The Bangladesh Garment Manufacturers and Exporters Association (BGMEA) – the manufacturers' professional body – was concerned about the US$3.18 billion worth of order cancellations that affected 1,150 factories. Between March and June 2020, Bangladesh lost US$4.9 billion worth of apparel orders compared against the same period in 2019. Members of BGMEA produce apparel including shirts, T-shirts, jackets, sweaters and trousers, which are mostly shipped to Europe, the US and Canada. Clothes with tags stating 'Made in Bangladesh' give Bangladesh a new identity; however, the tags and that identity do not show the toll on the workers that produce that apparel.

After the detection of the coronavirus, the government and the BGMEA have advised garment and knitwear factories to continue production with proper protection for workers if they have orders to deliver. The workers were asked to go to their villages after the declaration of the lockdown on 26 March 2020. But in April, despite the continuation of the lockdown and shutdown of transport, garment workers were contacted by management via SMS to return to their factories in April. RMG workers had to walk more than 100 kilometres from their villages to reach the factories in Dhaka, fearing otherwise they will lose their jobs as well as their outstanding pay. Once they arrived in Dhaka, a notice hanging on the factory told them that the lockdown had been extended, so they had to return to their villages.

Researchers pointed out that

such chaotic mobility of workers indicates a discrepancy between the owners' pledge to ensuring safety for workers and their actions in reality. To the owners as well as the state, workers' lives are not as important as profit. Besides, functioning labour unions that could take initiatives to support workers do not exist. (Luthfa, 2020)

RMG layoffs

Almost every day since April 2020 workers have taken to the streets demanding their wages or protesting job cuts and factory shutdowns, despite the COVID-19 pandemic.

Layoffs in the RMG sector started in April 2020. In 55 factories, 25,000 workers were laid off without receiving the pay they were owed. These workers had worked in the factory for at least one year. (Banglanews24, 2020)

The workers were given no notice of the layoffs. The factory Sigma Fashion Ltd declared it was closed until 5 May 2020. This factory had 1,200 workers. On 24 April 2020, 709 workers (60 per cent) were laid off without any prior notice. Fahima, a sewing operator, reported that on 16 April they were paid the money they were owed but they had to sign 15 papers without knowing what they were for. These workers could not leave their homes in Dhaka as they had three months of overdue rental payments. These workers had no option but to protest against the layoffs (Dainik Amader Shomoy, 2020).

By August 2020, the number of RMG workers that had been laid off since April reached 324,684 according to a study by the Bangladesh Institute of Labour Studies (BILS). The report revealed that more than 1,900 RMG factories were shut down or their workers were laid off during this time (*Dhaka Tribune*, 2020b).

About 26,500 garment workers were fired by 87 factories without following labour laws since the outbreak of the novel coronavirus and were deprived of getting their due wages and fair compensation (The Business Standard, 2020). The BILS study found that 80 per cent of laid-off workers had no savings, while 27 per cent had reduced their food expenses as monthly wages became irregular during the pandemic. However, they were not any better off before the pandemic. A previous BILS study in 2019 found 56 per cent of RMG workers procured their essential commodities on credit, and 72 per cent could not get proper medical treatment due to low wages, while the pandemic amplified their crises even more (*Dhaka Tribune*, 2020b).

The effects of the economic slowdown caused by the COVID-19 pandemic resulted in job and salary cuts, job uncertainty, sudden layoffs and shutdown of factories. The RMG workers were thrown into uncertainty that nobody was taking responsibility for. Many factories were running their production without complying with the COVID-19 health guidelines. The government had taken no initiatives to prevent layoffs in factories.

> Parents working in a garment factory located in Gazipur (near Dhaka) had to sell their newborn baby, as they could not pay the hospital bill of BDT 25 000 ($295). The father of the newborn baby said that they could not manage hospital bills as the garment factory, where both husband and wife used to work, was closed because of the COVID-19 pandemic. However, the local police rescued the baby and returned it to their parents. (*The Daily Prothom Alo*, 2020)

Returned to their villages, then what?

According to a Bangladesh Institute of Development Studies (BIDS) survey, about 13 per cent of people have become unemployed in the country due to the COVID-19 pandemic. The survey found negative effects on employment, income and expenditures, especially for those on low incomes. The report indicated that 19.23 per cent with those with an income below Tk5,000 reported that their income was reduced by 75 per cent, while 23.31 per cent with income of Tk5000–15000 reported an income reduction of 50 per cent relative to the previous month's income (*Daily Star*, 2020).

The informal sector was the hardest hit, with an estimated 80 per cent of workers becoming unemployed. As many businesses were closing, a very large number of workers were not able to return to their jobs. Many people were reverse migrating from urban to rural areas. Households experienced serious financial stress causing a sharp decline in household consumption (*Financial Express*, 2020).

Although rural young men and women were invited to the capital city Dhaka to work in the RMG industries, they never adapted to city life. They lived in slums and shanties but only to sleep at night after working hours and for weekends. A week off (whether through choice or factory closure) always led to leaving the city, because city life is too expensive. Therefore, when RMG factory owners decided to keep the factories closed until 14 April 2020, all RMG workers left Dhaka amid the shutdown of public transport. All the exit points in Dhaka were crowded with people looking for the limited transport available. Going home was difficult for the workers because of the stigma associated with COVID-19 deaths, although only nine deaths had been recorded by that time. Police restrictions on entering or leaving Dhaka added further woe to the workers.

Among married RMG workers, according to an ILO study, nearly half work in the RMG sector. Nearly 36.5 per cent of couples work in the same factory and 63.5 per cent in different factories. These couples kept their children, almost from infancy, back in their village homes with grandparents. They were being raised in the villages with money sent back by their parents (ILO and UN Women, 2020).

Due to the layoffs, the garment workers who went back to their villages faced an environment different to that they had experienced before. These garment workers used to support their families financially. The following case studies give a picture of how these workers were received in their villages.

Case 1

Amirul Islam and Jesmin Khatun used to work in the same garment factory in Gazipur, a sub-urban industrial zone near Dhaka. Since 2015, Amirul, the husband, had worked as a helper at a salary of Tk6700 and Jesmin joined the same factory in 2019 at a salary of Tk4500 in the production section as an apprentice. The couple has a 7-month-old son, whom they left with their parents in the village. The factory was closed during the pandemic and they were not paid. They had difficulty in paying for food and rent. They finally gave up and left Dhaka for their village in the Pabna district.

In the village, Amirul did not find any work. He wanted to work in the fields, but due to lack of skill he could earn Tk 50 per day compared with Tk350 per day for skilled workers. He did not want to do this work anymore. He planned to buy an Auto-rickshaw at Tk90,000, which he had to borrow from Jesmin's father, an indirect way of taking a dowry. The couple did not feel welcomed by the family as they could not contribute anymore. Jesmin did not have any work to do. She is now looking after her son.

Case 2

Rahela Begum, aged 20, had a good job as an operator in the RMG factory. She married Zahir, a colleague in the same factory. Rahela earned a salary of Tk9,000; with overtime, it rose to Tk12,000 per month. Zahir used to get Tk15,000 including overtime. The couple was happy with their earnings. They lived in a house with rent costing Tk4,000 per month. Both of them lost their jobs after the pandemic. When they were laid off, they did not receive their full monthly salary. Together they received Tk16,000.

Without jobs, the couple realized that it would be difficult to live in Dhaka. They decided to go to Mymensingh, and stay in Zahir's parents' house. Rahela could not stay there for more than 20 days. Her father-in-law is a day labourer who could not find any work during the lockdown. Zahir was also unable to find work. The savings they had were spent on outstanding house rent and on food after they arrived in the village. Her father-in-law asked Rahela to stay and eat separately. Zahir asked her to go to her father's house in another district, Lalmonirhat.

Rahela's parents are also very poor, earning little from wage work. Rahela had been staying in Lalmonirhat for seven months (as of November, 2020). Zahir no longer contacted her. The only job she could find was in a Zarda-Gul (smokeless tobacco) factory, and she earned Tk70 per day. She bought rice and some vegetables with that money. This work was quite hazardous for her, but she had to earn money to avoid starvation.

Case 3

Masuma (24) went to Dhaka to work in a knitwear factory as a helper at the age of 19 in 2015. Other girls from her village in Chapainababganj were also working in the factories. As a helper, she got a very low wage, but she learnt the work of an operator within 6 months. She then shifted to another factory and got a better job in the quality control section. With overtime, her monthly earnings were Tk12,000. She went to the factory at 8 am and worked until 8 pm (if there was overtime). During the shipment of the garments, the workers had to work until 3 am. They had to work like this for 15 days a month.

Yet she was happy to do the work. She sent Tk3000 per month to her mother, which was mostly used by her brother.

In the factory, she met Jasimuddin and got married in 2018. He was not happy with his job and the salary, so he resigned. Masuma bought a tailoring machine costing Tk15,000 for him so that he can do some work independently. The couple lived in a rented house at Tk4000 per month. Masuma used to send money to her in-laws living in Cumilla.

Masuma got pregnant in March 2020. In late March, the factory declared a lockdown for 15 days. She along with her husband went to Cumilla in her in-law's house. They loved her and she was happy there.

After 15 days, the workers were called back to Dhaka, she came to Dhaka almost walking and taking short rides, covering 100 kilometres. Unfortunately, when she reported to the factory, she was told that 'she was no more required'. Along with her, 227 workers were laid off. She was given three months of salary in arrears (Tk29934). She did not receive payment for her overtime.

Masuma returned again to her in-laws in Cumila. Her husband's tailoring business was also closed. They took all their furniture and other belongings and went to Cumilla. This time they were not welcomed. She spent all her savings on their food and other necessities. One day her father-in-law asked her to leave and go to her father's house. When she contacted her brother, he said 'you are pregnant. It will be too much pressure on us to keep you. It will also be a social problem as the society in her village did not see her husband at all'. It was settled that her husband would go with her and let people know that she is legitimately married and pregnant.

She could not stay with her brother. She is now living with her sister. Her husband went back to Dhaka with his tailoring work but he was not earning enough to bring his wife. Masuma was staying at her sister's house until she gave birth.

Case 4

Maherun (40) worked in the garment factory. She came to Dhaka at the age of 18. She started work in a Korean-owned factory. After working for 20 years and 5 months, she lost her job during the lockdown. She went to her village for the initial lockdown in March–April. When she came back to Dhaka, she found that she had been laid off. When she asked why she lost the job, the management said that she was too old for such work and she had weak eye vision.

She had a daughter and a son. They were students in college and school, and she had to pay for their education. So she could not leave Dhaka, but staying was very expensive. She looked for work as a house maid, but no such work was available in the pandemic.

She went back to her village in Patuakhali but found that there was also no work there. She gave her savings of Tk36,000 to her husband for his fish business.

References

ADB (2020) *COVID-19 and the Ready-Made Garments Industry in Bangladesh: COVID-19 Active Response and Expenditure Support (CARES) Program*, RRP BAN 54180.

Banglanews24 (2020) **দেশের ৫৫টি পোশাক কারখানায় ছাঁটাই হয়েছে ২৫ হাজার শ্রমিক**, Banglanews24, 23 April. www.banglanews24. com/economics-business/news/bd/784557.details

The Business Standard (2020) '3 lakh RMG workers lost job in pandemic', *The Business Standard*, 27 August. https://tbsnews.net/ economy/rmg/3-lakh-rmg-workers-lost-job-pandemic-125206

The Daily Prothom Alo (2020) 'Parents in a garment factory sell their newborn baby', *The Daily Prothom Alo*, 2 May.

Daily Star (2020) '13pc people lost jobs due to Covid-19 pandemic: BIDS survey, by UNB', *The Daily Star*, 25 June. www. thedailystar.net/business/13pc-people-lost-jobs-in-bangladesh-due-covid-19-pandemic-1920309

Dainik Amader Shomoy (2020) '**আশুলিয়ায় ছাঁটাইয়ের প্রতিবাদে পোশাক শ্রমিকদের বিক্ষোভ**', 25 April. www.dainikamade rshomoy.com/post/253469

Dhaka Tribune (2020a) '35–40% RMG workers in Bangladesh require eyeglasses, finds survey', *Dhaka Tribune*, 4 March. www.dhakatrib une.com/business/2020/03/04/35-40-rmg-workers-in-banglad esh-require-eyeglasses-finds-survey

Dhaka Tribune (2020b) 'Study: 325,000 RMG workers lost jobs due to pandemic', *Dhaka Tribune*, 29 August. www.dhakatribune.com/business/2020/08/29/study-325-000-rmg-workers-lose-jobs-due-to-pandemic

Dhaka Tribune (2020c) 'GAIN: Nearly half of RMG workforce malnourished', *Dhaka Tribune*, 29 September. www.dhakatribune.com/bangladesh/2020/09/29/gain-nearly-half-of-rmg-workforce-malnourished

Financial Express (2020) 'On Bangladesh GDP in the time of coronavirus', *Financial Express*, 5 September. https://thefinancialexpress.com.bd/views/reviews/on-bangladesh-gdp-in-the-time-of-coronavirus-1599314452

Government of Bangladesh (2015) *Statistical Pocket Book Bangladesh 2014*. Bangladesh Bureau of Statistics, Ministry of Planning, Government of Bangladesh.

ILO (2019) 'Improving working conditions in the readymade garment sector, Bangladesh baseline study January – May 2017, study South Asia Network for Economic Modeling (SANEM) for ILO'.

ILO and UN Women (2020) 'Issue Brief: Understanding the gender composition and experience of ready-made garment (RMG) workers in Bangladesh'. https://www.ilo.org/wcmsp5/groups/public/---asia/---ro-bangkok/---ilo-dhaka/documents/publication/wcms_754669.pdf

Khan, M.T. and Rahman, M.S. (eds) (2019) *Neoliberal Development in Bangladesh: People on the Margins*, The University Press.

Luthfa, S. (2020) 'Challenges of life and livelihood', *New Age*, 15 October. www.newagebd.net/article/118992/challenges-of-life-and-livelihood

New Age (2020) 'Number of female workers in RMG sector falling: surveys', *The New Age*, 25 December. www.newagebd.net/article/124375/number-of-female-workers-in-rmg-sector-falling-surveys

UBINIG (2020a) *Farming Community & Agriculture*, UBINIG Report Series # 1, April.

UBINIG (2020b) *Reinventing Agriculture: Need a Paradigm Shift to Agro-Ecological Principles*, COVID-19: UBINIG Report Series 3, 19 May.

UBINIG (2020c) *Pandemic and Public Health Challenges in Bangladesh*, UBINIG Report Series 4, 3 June.

UBINIG (2020d) *Jibon* or *Jibika*: The struggle for life and livelihood amid pandemic, October. www.ubinig.org

UBINIG (2020e) 'UBINIG Survey in Tangail, Pabna and Natore on the effects of COVID-19 on the small scale farmers', unpublished.

EIGHT

Mapping the Multiple Vulnerabilities of Domestic Workers During COVID-19: Reflections from India

Sabiha Hussain

Introduction

The informal sector in India represents 90 per cent of labour in the country (Government of India, 2018). The pandemic and its huge economic shock have only made the fragile situation worse for the informal sector. Several workers were stranded without work when the lockdown was imposed.

Domestic workers (DWs) are a part of the large 'informal' sector of urban economy and society in India. Over the past two decades, the population of DWs has emerged as the second largest urban informal workforce (Chen and Raveendran, 2012). According to the National Sample Survey (NSS) 68th round (July 2011–June 2012),[1] it is estimated that 413,000 workers work in the households of others, and an overwhelming 279,000 of this total are women.

Domestic workers during the pandemic

DWs are largely invisible, performing labour behind closed doors of private households and unprotected by national, state laws. Many tasks performed by them are not recognized as 'work', along with the larger social devaluation of women's domestic work and labour within families. Women dominate domestic work in Asia. In fact, up to 90 per cent of DWs are female and domestic work is now the most common occupation for women in the region.

When women DWs faced the imposition of lockdowns to control the spread of the novel coronavirus, their vulnerabilities were enhanced and this raised questions about policy and societal attitude towards them. The restriction on travel impacted their livelihood, income security and health, and they also faced increased violence by their partners, which made them the most vulnerable workers of the informal sector. This chapter addresses some of these issues.

Research design and methodology

This study is exploratory and responses were collected through an unstructured interview schedule from Delhi/ National Capital Region (NCR). A mixed method was used to collect data and, hence, the study is both qualitative and quantitative in nature. A sample of 100 respondents as representative of this group of workers, largely migrants, aged 18–45 was selected through purposive sampling. For in-depth case study, 10 percent of the total sample was taken. Special attention was given in sample selection to caste, communities, religion, region and age of the respondents for examining the intersectionality of their forms of vulnerabilities. However, the analysis of the data shows hardly any difference in their experiences.

Socioeconomic and demographic profile of domestic workers

Tables 8.1 to 8.9 detail certain socioeconomic and demographic features of the domestic workers that responded to the survey.

Table 8.1: Caste, % of respondents

Caste	% of respondents
General	49
Other Backward Castes	29
Scheduled Castes	13
Scheduled Tribes	9

Table 8.2: Marital status, % of respondents

Marital status	% of respondents
Married	74
Unmarried	8
Divorced/Separated	8
Widowed	10

Table 8.3: Religion, % of respondents

Religion	% of respondents
Hindu	60
Muslim	24
Christian	6
Other	10

Table 8.4: Education level, % of respondents

Education level	% of respondents
Illiterate	49
Primary (5th grade)	29
Primary (8th grade)	13
Senior secondary	9
Secondary	1

Table 8.5: Residence status, % of respondents

Residence status	% of respondents
Rented	62
Owned	38

Table 8.6: Monthly income, % of respondents

Monthly income	% of respondents
Less than INR3,000	14
INR3,000–5,000	28
INR5,000–8,000	33
INR8,000–10,000	16
More than INR10,000	9

Table 8.7: Length of migration, % of respondents

Length of migration	% of respondents
0–5 years	5
5–10 years	15
10–15 years	38
15–20 years	22
20+ years	20

Table 8.8: Reason for migration, % of respondents

Reason for migration	% of respondents
Employment	29
Business	2
Education	1
Marriage	28
After giving birth	14
Came with family	26

Table 8.9: Number of children per family, % of respondents

Number of children	% of respondents
One	23
Two	39
Three	23
More than three	11

Results and discussion

Impact of COVID-19 on work, livelihood and survival

Women's workforce participation in India was low due to social and cultural reasons at just 24 per cent, according to the Economic Survey 2017–18 (Government of India, 2017–18). However, due to the pandemic and subsequent lockdown, the suffering of DWs has increased in terms of livelihood and survival. The field data reveals that 56 per cent workers did not get their salary during lockdown, 26 per cent received half of their salary and 18 per cent got their salary after their rejoining (see Table 8.10). Thus, during lockdown they had to go through a difficult time in terms of livelihood and survival.

For 8 per cent workers, employers stopped paying their salaries due to their own financial circumstances. Amid the lockdown, these workers did not only lose their source of livelihood and regular flow of income but also there was a continuous uncertainty of reemployment for them. The situation was further aggravated as many of them were migrants and did not have ration cards and other necessary documents to access the benefits of the government support scheme. This had made them more vulnerable to food insecurity.

The majority (69 per cent) stated that after losing their livelihoods having even one meal a day was difficult. Live-in DWs faced more difficulties as during lockdown most continued to work in confinement with their employers for longer hours due to closures of schools and offices.

Table 8.10: Effect of COVID-19 on major source of income, % of respondents

Effect	% of respondents
Cut in salary	26
No salary	56
Pay after returning to work	18

In response to how they coped with the crisis of food and economic hardships, the majority (58 per cent) said that during pandemic initially there were two meals a day but as the lockdown continued, there was scarcity of food and they had to survive on one meal. Rent was paid by taking loans from private moneylenders on high interest rates. Hardly any help was provided by the government to meet the demand of food. NGOs provided food parcels.

After lockdown ended, 48 per cent of workers were yet to find a job, 27 per cent were allowed to work but in not more than two houses, and 15 per cent were working in one house only with certain conditions and always looked on with suspicion, even for a little coughing or sneezing.

Mary, 28, recalls the sudden lockdown had put the whole family in a state of shock. Her husband lost his livelihood. They could manage with their savings for two months. Her employer refused to help. Finding no jobs, they went back their native place by borrowing money from a private moneylender. Now she is back and trying to get a job. Others have more or less the same narratives to share.

Reemployment after lockdown

At the time of interview, 57 per cent of respondents were jobless. Nevertheless, those who had got a job after lockdown had to make compromises.

Table 8.11: Employment status after the first lockdown, % of respondents

Employment status	% of respondents
No work	57
Employed for the last three months	20
Conditional return to employment	17
Lower salary	14

Table 8.11 reveals that 17 per cent had conditions placed on their return to work, including: they had to leave if they showed even slight symptoms of a cough or cold; they could work only in one house; they had to change their clothes before starting work; no conversations were allowed during work; mobile phones had to be kept outside. Also 14 per cent were working on lower pay than previously – they had no option because they were the only earning family member. Twenty per cent of respondents got their salary for at least three months of the lockdown, although the lockdown lasted almost six months.

Sunita, 39, working in three houses, lost her job during lockdown. She somehow survived on dry rations given by her employer in the beginning of lockdown but worried about the monthly rent and other regular maintenance expenditure. After lockdown she managed to get work but only in one house as per the regulations at that time and her husband is yet to get a job. Her income is not enough to meet the basic needs of the family.

Facilities provided by the government during lockdown

In response to a survey question on the government's Jan Dhan Yojna[2,3] scheme (economic empowerment scheme), rations from the government under a public distribution system and COVID-19 protection kits, it was found that 19 per cent of respondents received money under the Jan Dhan scheme. They could not access the ration due to lockdown. However, 53 per cent of the women surveyed said that they had no access to any of these facilities irrespective of caste, communities and religion.

Despite the advisory issued by the National Human Rights Commission (NHRC) to the government on protecting women's rights during the pandemic (*The Hindu*, 2020), to provide sanitary napkins and iron/folic acid supplements as essential items and through the Rajiv Gandhi Scheme for Empowerment of Adolescent Girls and *Rashtriya Kishor Swasthya Karyakram* (Jolly et al, 2014), 56 per cent of the respondents stated that getting sanitary napkins and supplements for pregnant women during lockdown was the biggest problem. Most of the women surveyed (92 per cent) had accessed the provision by NGOs of grains, COVID-19 protection kits, sanitary napkins, medicine and baby food. This raises a serious question about the responsibility of the state.

The impact of COVID-19 on women's health

The increased amount of care work during the pandemic has become a major source of stress and hence affects the health of women workers. Zhan (2005) showed that, before the pandemic, women spent 5–10 more hours per week on providing care to children and the elderly than men. We tried to explore the issue of the increased burden of household and care work, alongside pregnancy, family planning, gynaecological and mental health, caused by the COVID-19 lockdown.

Two-thirds of women respondents stated that since all family members were at home, they had to shoulder a disproportionate responsibility for care giving and housework, which had increased their physical and mental stress. However, 26 per cent responded negatively and 8 per cent did not respond.

Table 8.12: Respondents' use of government support during the pandemic, % of respondents

Government support	% of respondents
Jan Dan Yojna	15
Rations from public distribution system	20
COVID protection kit	12
None	53

Table 8.13: Respondents' use of NGO support during the pandemic, % of respondents

NGO support	% of respondents
Packed food	32
COVID protection kit	28
Medicine and baby food	22
None	8

Maintaining hygiene and cleanliness

During the field visit to the slum, it was found that hygiene conditions were very poor with a common water supply and shared toilets; therefore, washing hands and clothes at regular intervals and adhering to safety measures was not viable. On the one hand, the workers had lost their livelihoods; on the other, living conditions and maintaining COVID-19 measures were making these workers' lives even more woeful.

Thus, we tried to find out how they maintained health and hygiene (see Table 8.14). It was found that the most popularly adopted measure was maintaining social distancing (42 per cent), followed by personal cleanliness (20 per cent) like washing hands and clothes, but not other recommended COVID-19 safety measures such as using sanitizers, gloves or a mask, though they used their *chunni* (scarf) as medical grade ones were costly. However, 20 per cent had taken no measures

Table 8.14: Personal hygiene and safety measures during COVID-19, % of respondents

Measure	% of respondents
Social distancing	42
Personal cleanliness	30
No measure	20
No response	8

to maintain health and hygiene during the pandemic due to the financial crisis.

Pregnancy and family planning

Another issue addressed in this research is that of pregnancy, family planning gynaecological problems and mental health.

Table 8.15 indicates that the major problem during the pandemic was of non-availability of contraceptives (30 per cent), followed by non-availability of sanitary napkins (20 per cent), gynaecological issues (12 per cent), and unwanted pregnancies (10 per cent). A few respondents (3 per cent) used home remedies to abort unwanted pregnancies, resulting in more complications, and causing stress and frailty. The majority faced post-partum problems, and a lack of antenatal and post-natal care due to the lockdown and monetary problems.

During lockdown, Hajra, 35, had to bear the abuse of her husband and unprotected sex resulted in pregnancy. There was no help of any kind from the government in terms of providing medicine or birth control methods.

Asha, 29, had a similar narrative, being burdened with household work, forced sex (a refusal to have sex resulted in physical abuse) and having to carry an unwanted pregnancy.

Table 8.15: Reproductive health issues during COVID-19, % of respondents

Issue	% of respondents
Unwanted pregnancy	10
Non-availability of birth control	30
Non-availability of sanitary napkins	20
Gynaecological problem	12
No problem	28

Antenatal check-ups and delivery problems during COVID-19

Issues around antenatal checks during pregnancy and the place of delivery of the child were also explored in the study. During lockdown, 18 women had their baby delivered and of these, ten had a home delivery helped by traditional birth attendants, as the women were afraid of going to hospital and bearing the cost of private hospitals/clinics was out of the question. Due to lockdown, there was no last trimester check-up. Some of the women continued to suffer gynaecological problems caused by childbirth (having been attended by a traditional birth attendant) but could not afford to visit a hospital. It was found during interviews that the impact of lockdown was more severe on pregnant and lactating women, as there was shortage of food in the family.

Women and mental health

During COVID-19 workers were suffering from high degrees of anxiety and fears, and were in need of psychosocial support (Government of India, 2020). In addition there was also an increase in the feeling of loneliness, causing mental issues (Nelson, 2020).

Table 8.16: Mental health problems experienced during COVID-19, % of respondents

Mental health problem	% of respondents
Anxiety	20
Stress	16
Sleeplessness	13
Anger	8
Loneliness	15
No problem	28

We asked the women if they had faced any kind of mental health issues during the sudden lockdown – which had resulted in financial crisis and food insecurity – and how they had coped with this situation. The data reveals that 72 per cent of the respondents faced or were still facing mental health issues, which they termed as *Dimaghi Preshani* (mental stress) arising out of job loss, quarantine rules, economic hardship, domestic violence and certain reproductive health issues (see Table 8.16).

More precisely, anxiety was reported by 20 per cent, mainly caused by job loss and economic hardship, followed by stress (16 per cent), due to the increased workload leading to an emotional burden on women; 15 per cent reported loneliness and 13 per cent reported sleeplessness due to stress of survival and reemployment. However, 28 per cent responded negatively to this question. Looking at the greater percentage of women reporting mental health issues, we further probed the respondents as to what did they do to address this issue (see Table 8.17).

It was found that 40 per cent tried to keep themselves busy with household work, 26 per cent talked to friends by phone, 20 per cent cried and 10 per cent spent time in prayer. With the majority in our sample being illiterate, the women explained in their own terminology and understanding the various mental

Table 8.17: Mental health coping mechanisms, % of respondents

Coping mechanism	% of respondents
Crying	20
Keeping busy in work	40
Talking to friends	26
Prayer	10
Sleeping	4

health problems they faced and the strategies they used to cope with the situation. Some of the women's narratives about stress, fear and anxiety were captured irrespective of caste, religion, communities and regional boundaries.

Ramkali, aged 36: "What would happen to my children as we were running short of food, continuous threat to vacate the house, and there was no help from the government or the employer."

Sohiala, 32: "I had many sleepless night thinking of no job and there was no hope of getting job during unlock. All these had increased irritation and verbal fight with each other that is very stressful."

Women's response and experiences of domestic violence during COVID-19

Preliminary reports from around the world have suggested there was a 30 to 50 per cent increase in domestic violence during the pandemic (Bradbury–Jones and Isham, 2020). India has reported a 50 per cent rise in domestic violence cases. A National Commission for Women (NCW) report showed a total of 800 complaints were received of various crimes against women, out of which 40 per cent constituted domestic violence (Tomar and Mohanty, 2020).

Table 8.18: Experience of domestic violence during the COVID-19 lockdown, % of respondents

Experience of domestic violence	% of respondents
Yes	82
No	18

We wanted to know from the women whether they faced violence during the pandemic, and if so, the types, the reasons, the frequency and if they sought help.

Table 8.18 reveals that 82 per cent of the women irrespective of caste, class, religion and regional boundaries reported domestic violence. The reasons include: loss of job(s); increased household work; living with the abuser; denial of sexual intercourse; and shortage of alcohol for their husbands. Severity further increased due to the stronger grip of patriarchy and the culture of silence.

It is also important to mention that due to lockdown and social distancing the support systems provided by the government became limited for the victims of domestic violence. Moreover, they were bound to live with abusive partners who hurt them physically and emotionally:

Shomona (Scheduled caste community), 28: "There was an increase in verbal and physical abuse as during lockdown he could not get alcohol. He used to beat her almost every day in front of her children but she could not go to police, not to her relatives, no idea about helpline, hence she had to live with the abuser."

Anisa, 34 recalls, "those were the worst days of my life, we were without food for almost two days: loss of job and hardship of survival had made my husband more irritated resulted in physical abuse; I could not go anywhere nor sought protection outside; no idea of helpline and there was no money to recharge mobile."

Shabana, 30, shares "he used to physically abuse her before lockdown also but the frequency of abuse increased and same with sexual intercourse resulting in unwanted pregnancy. Resistance resulted into physical abuse. She was not aware of any helpline; no money to recharge her mobile. She further adds, there is no point in seeking help, as I have to live with the abuser."

Shobha, 34, stated "Earlier also I was physically abused but during lockdown it was increased even for a small thing he used to shout at me and beat me but due to lockdown I kept quiet."

Women were asked to explain what kind of violence they faced during pandemic (see Table 8.19). Physical violence was the most common (48 per cent; slapping, pushing against the wall, pulling of hair), followed by abusive language and the throwing of utensils or water on their faces (28 per cent). Sexual abuse like forced sex was reported by 11 per cent and emotional abuse by 13 per cent (demands to stop talking, making fun of their behaviour, face or complexions).

When asked about reporting violence, 44 per cent did not know about legal recourse or helplines (most were aged 35 upwards); 23 per cent knew about shelter homes, especially the younger age group; 18 per cent about helplines; and 12 per cent about NGO support. However, the majority did not report the violence due to quarantine rules and because they had to live with their abusers so any complaint would have further increased their problems.

Table 8.20 shows that 62 per cent of women did not inform anyone about the violence against them, while 14 per cent

Table 8.19: Types of violence experienced, % of respondents

Type of violence	% of respondents
Verbal abuse	28
Physical abuse	48
Emotional abuse	13
Sexual abuse	11

Table 8.20: Agencies or individuals informed about domestic violence, % of respondents

Agency/Individual	% of respondents
None	62
Neighbour	4
Police	4
Didn't face domestic violence	18
Other family member	6
Friends	4
Helpline	2

informed friends, a neighbour or family members. Only 6 per cent called a helpline or the police but received no response. When asked what they did when the violence was happening, interestingly, 55 per cent kept quiet, 24 per cent shouted and cried, 11 per cent hit back to defend themselves, and 10 per cent locked themselves in a room to save themselves.

Voices and expectations of domestic workers

Having analysed the data, it is pertinent to discuss what these workers wanted in terms of their job, health and to curb violence, especially in a situation such as the pandemic. They were asked to express their expectations of their employer, Residents Welfare Association (RWA) and the government. First, they stated that the societies in Delhi/NCR had completely ignored and stigmatized DWs when the lockdown was abruptly announced. It was disheartening and disappointing when they found out about notifications issued overnight banning their entry from the vicinity of the housing society. These societies completely ignored and stigmatized DWs, causing joblessness, food insecurity and increased violence in the family. DWs would have liked at least a few weeks' notice before being refused entry to the households where they worked, and wanted the government to issue an advisory to employers to ensure advance payment of salaries. This could have saved DWs from hunger and mental trauma. It was also stated by the respondents that the RWA and employers should call them back to work without any prejudice and conditions, and that wage compensation should be given to them for the lockdown period. They were of the strong view that they must not be seen as carriers of the virus and discriminated in terms of using the lift, which was observed in a few buildings in Delhi/NCR. They also demanded that essential items such as sanitizers, mask and gloves must be provided by the employer, as they cannot afford to buy them. It is important to mention that these workers were aware about the workers union and expressed their desire to have a DWs union led by women to meet their requirements along with other officials or members in each society or apartment, especially the younger women. They also put forth the idea that there must be one representative from the DWs working in the respective societies and with the RWA for any decision-making processes related to these workers.

When asked what they expect from the government, they strongly stated that the provision of immediate relief to DWs through cash transfers (Jan Dhan Yojna) should be continued until the pandemic ends and that there should be less paperwork. They also stated that there is an urgent need for the government or other regulatory body to issue an advisory to all resident welfare associations and employers to create a mechanism for work security or unconditional reemployment without any prejudice, and to provide wage compensation for these workers so that their safety and job security is ensured. They strongly felt the need for legislation that ensures the livelihood and other benefits of workers beyond the pandemic and other natural calamities.

Claire Hobden stated that 'The COVID-19 crisis has exposed the particular vulnerability of informal domestic workers, emphasizing the urgent need to ensure they are effectively included in labour and social protection.' She further said that 'This disproportionately affects women who make up the vast majority of domestic workers worldwide' (Neetha and Palriwala, 2011).

Vulnerabilities of domestic workers: reviewing the policy gaps

The abuse and exploitation of DWs remains rampant mainly due to the lack of legal or regulatory regimes to protect them, and the absence of adequate mechanisms for redress in law or policy. The other reason behind such an unstable work atmosphere is the power dynamic. DWs are not recognized as 'workers' in society, and their contribution is not acknowledged to be 'productive work'. This unrecognized and unacknowledged contribution affects women workers even more adversely.

A brief review of the policies shows that DWs have been sidelined from state policies and laws many times (India Together, 2020). In 1959, a private member's bill was initiated to regulate the deteriorating condition of DWs: the Domestic Workers (Condition of Services) Bill was moved in the Rajya Sabha, but failed to be enacted. More private members' bills were introduced in the Lok Sabha in 1972 and 1977 respectively, which too lapsed. In 1974, the Committee on Status of Women in India recommended the government address the condition of DWs; the recommendation was neglected. In 1988, a recommendation was made by the Statutory National Commission of Self-Employed Women and Women in the Informal Sector for the registration of workers to protect them. The 1989 House Workers Bill was also not enacted. There was an attempt to bring about specific legislation meant for DWs by the National Commission for Women. This was the Domestic Workers Welfare and Social Security Act 2010, but the Bill was never passed. In 2016, Shashi Tharoor introduced the Domestic Workers' Welfare

Bill. This Bill too has not seen execution so there exists no statute or legislation applicable to DWs per se.

Two other legislations – the Unorganized Workers Social Security Act 2008 and the Sexual Harassment of Women at Workplace (Prevention, Prohibition and Redressal) Act 2013 – include DWs, but do not address their specific vulnerabilities.

The question remains: What were the reasons for not enacting these bills? One of the major reasons is the 1926 Trade Unions Act according to which workers engaged in personal service cannot be considered as 'workmen'. In other words, labour legislations in India show that DWs are not included in the scope of several labour laws because of the restrictive definitions of 'workman', 'employer' or 'establishment'. Further, with the workplace being a private household or private establishment, that excludes DWs coverage from existing laws.

A few states like Andhra Pradesh, Bihar, Chhattisgarh, Jharkhand, Karnataka, Kerala, Maharashtra, Odisha, Rajasthan and Tamil Nadu have taken several steps to improve working conditions of DWs by providing access to Social Security Schemes. For example, the state of Jharkhand passed its Private Placement Agencies and Domestic Workers (Regulation) Bill 2016 to regulate the functioning of placement agencies and affording legal protection to DWs.

Filling the lacuna

First and foremost, there is a need to change the legal definition of 'domestic worker' as this would help in securing the rights of DWs. For example, households must be treated as workplaces and not 'private spaces'. The state must recognize DWs as essential service providers by regulating their working and living conditions and by placing restrictions on work that is physically or psychologically demanding. The issue of legislation protecting migrant DWs from abusive or fraudulent practices, especially by private agencies, is equally important and hence, addressing the liability of private agencies by creating an appropriate authority is necessary.

At the policy level, the bill drafted by the National Platform for Domestic Workers (the Domestic Workers Regulation of Work and Social Security Bill 2016, which went to the government in January 2020), must be passed and implemented so that in case of any natural calamity or pandemic DWs can be protected. The easy registration of DWs as 'workers' under the Labour Department through already existing systems is urgently required.

Last but not the least, as pointed out by Unni Krishnan, Humanitarian Director of War Child, in India Together (2020):

> The government must not look at the pandemic as a mere health emergency. It has to immediately take steps to stop domestic violence and child abuse. The top leadership must quickly articulate the role of the police in stopping it. Abusers need to be checkmated immediately. Otherwise, its impacts will have serious consequences. In many cases, it will lead to irreversible damage shattering many lives. Years later, women and children who were subjected to violence, will continue to relive the trauma.

Conclusion

To conclude, at both the policy and societal levels these DWs were the most vulnerable during the COVID-19 pandemic lockdown. The state largely failed to perform its responsibilities in protecting the vulnerabilities of these workers. Civil societies played a significant role in supporting these workers with relief packages, programmes and schemes. Reemployment was a big issue, as workers were seen as carriers of the virus, and faced discrimination and stigma during the pandemic even after the first lockdown ended. Hence, more measures need to be taken by the government and local administration as many workers remain out of the fold.

Although India is a signatory to ILO's 189th convention, known as Convention on the Domestic Workers, this has yet to be ratified. There is an urgent need to ratify it as this Convention mandates daily and weekly rest hours, a minimum wage requirement, a choice of place to live and freedom to spend their leave as they wish. At the policy level, only central law can meet the requirements of regulating DWs. If the state takes up its responsibility, the degree of their vulnerabilities would decline, especially during natural calamities or pandemic-like situations.

Notes

[1] http://microdata.gov.in/nada43/index.php/catalog/127/study-descript ion#:~:text=The%20NSS%2068th.%20round%20carried%20out%20 during%20July%272011,Household%20Consumer%20Expenditure%20 and%20%28ii%29%20Employment%20and%20Unemployment.

[2] Pradhanmantri Jan Dhan Yojana was launched in 2014. Under this scheme, the government helped to raise women's ownership of bank accounts. Women Jan Dhan account holders get INR500 per month for three months. An overdraft facility of Rs. 5000 is provided to one account in the household. This facility is usually provided to the woman in the house.

[3] In 2014, the Ministry of Health and Family Welfare launched a health programme (Rashtriya Kishor Swasthya Karyakram) for adolescents aged 10–19 to target their nutrition, reproductive health and substance abuse, among other issues.

References

Bradbury-Jones, C. and Isham, L. (2020) 'The pandemic paradox: The consequences of COVID-19 on domestic violence', *Journal of Clinical Nursing*, 29(13–14): 2047–49.

Chen, M.A. and Raveendran, G. (2012) 'Urban employment in India: Recent trends and patterns', *Margin: The Journal of Applied Economic Research*, 6(2): 159–79.

Chigateri, S., Zaidi, M. and Ghosh, A. (2016) *Locating the Processes of Policy Change in the Context of Anti-Rape and Domestic Worker Mobilisations in India*. United Nations Research Institute for Social Development.

Government of India (2017–18) 'Economic Survey 2017–18, Volume d1', Ministry of Finance. https://mofapp.nic.in/economicsurvey/economicsurvey/index.html

Government of India (2018) 'Periodic Labour Force Survey, 2017–18', Ministry of Statistics and Programme Implementation. https://mospi.gov.in/documents/213904/0/nsc_AR_2017-18.pdf/c1e8cf40-6c6f-d105-7e7b-216b05ebef1d?t=159517030447

Government of India (2020) 'Psychosocial issues among migrants during COVID-19', Ministry of Health and Family Welfare. www.mohfw.gov.in/pdf/RevisedPsychosocialissuesofmigrants COVID19.pdf

The Hindu (2020) 'National Human Rights Commission Advisory to Government on Women's Rights during Pandemic, Special Correspondence', *The Hindu*, 8 October.

Hobden, C. (2020) 'Livelihoods of more than 55 million domestic workers at risk due to COVID-19', International Labour Organization, 16 June.

India Together (2020) 'Domestic violence rising during pandemic', 17 March. http://indiatogether.org/domestic-violence-women

Jolly, S., Griffith, K. A., DeCastro, R., Stewart, A., Ubel, P. and Jagsi, R. (2014) 'Gender differences in time spent on parenting and domestic responsibilities by high-achieving young physician-researchers', *Annals of Internal Medicine*, 160(5): 344–53.

Neetha, N. and Palriwala, R. (2011) 'The absence of state law: domestic workers in India', *Canadian Journal of Women and the Law*, 23(1): 97–119. https://muse.jhu.edu/article/433408

Tomar, R. and Mohanty, P.C. (2020) 'Tackling the shadow pandemic of rising domestic violence', *The New Indian Express*, 19 October. www.newindianexpress.com/opinions/2020/oct/19/tackling-the-shadow-pandemic-of-rising-domestic-violence-2212123.html

Zhan, H.J. (2005) 'Aging, health care, and elder care: perpetuation of gender inequalities in China', *Health Care for Women International*, 26(8): 693–712.

PART III

Lives Under Lockdown

NINE

Offshore: Lockdown Topographies[1]

Suvendrini Perera

In the annals of COVID-19, walking narratives already have their own special subset. This is a virus walk-story, a type of wandering in place that yet ranges across other times and geographies.

Walking, as Michel de Certeau (1994 [1998]) noted, is a rhetoric. The selection of a path is an act of composition akin to the turning of a phrase. A style of walking, like style in writing, 'connotes a singular', a 'way of being in the world' and a particular 'processing of the symbolic' (161–2). The walking rhetorics of this brief essay set a course across land, river and sea, at a crossroads of topographies and temporalities. Its turns, returns and detours encompass sheep and sea eagles, prison islands, a limestone rise; all manner of boats. Along its perambulations, another geography, strange, ancient and implacable, rises through the brittle lines of a small 19th-century settler colonial town set hard against the coastline of the Indian Ocean; sounds through its unsettled and shifting toponymies, Noongar, British, Australian.

Week 1, Day 4

It is only days now, and already the rhythm of our daily life has adapted to the unthinkable. Morning and evening we make our way, our small, interdependent, interspecies cluster: two canines, two humans, bound to one another by our shared intimacies and newly discovered vulnerabilities. Shrouded in our invisible pod, already, by reflex, we turn into a collective huddle as others approach, with only a small acknowledgement – a yelp, a namaste – across the width of the street. Almost overnight, the mundane practice of our walks has acquired new inflections: in an economy of lockdown, it seems, a dog to be walked represents a new type of currency. Is it this unexpected twist, this subtle rebalancing of needs at both ends of a leash, that adds a surreal quality to our stepping out onto silent streets?

Without the usual traffic sounds, our walks feel unreal. There is a translucent immateriality to the hush of this perfect transitional weather, the soft blue skies and red flowers that mark the season of Djeran. Our morning walks take us across Tuckfield Oval and down the levelled stages of the rise to the banks of the Derbarl Yerrigan. On flattened ground cut into the limestone, tucked out of sight of Canning Highway and looking down on the river, a small family (a woman, kids, a dog) has set up camp under the thick spread of a Moreton Bay fig tree, doubtless staying clear of the bizarre round-ups that are placing the unhoused under guard in four-star hotels.

At dusk, as we retrace our steps, we can see lights from their fire and the sway of a paper lantern. Along the Derbarl Yerrigan, the tide has started to go out, although dolphins still leap in the distance. Closer in, the swans for whom the interlopers named this place are starting to come ashore. Swan River Colony, a failed name soon to be replaced by a brutally serviceable one: Western Australia. To European eyes the black swan was a contradiction in terms, like much of the antipodes, an upturning or inversion of the natural order of things. The receding tide reveals them planted here on webbed feet, a solid black line, standing their ground.

Week 3, Day 5

Our walks set the tempo of our days, though one day is not so different from another. Our morning course takes us invariably past Rifle Cottage and Gun House, stationed side by side, with Gun House on slightly larger and higher ground, as befits the Commander's residence. On the other side of the oval, where once there might have been a parade ground, are the Artillery Barracks.

Prisons, asylums and barracks define the limits of the old town: the architectural signature of occupation. Cantonment Hill rises above, a name redolent of childhood walks in Colombo, another Indian Ocean port city of the British Empire. A signal station, now abandoned, sits at the crest. Quarried relentlessly for its limestone and riddled with tunnels and small paths, the hill is still home to small wildlife and imported pests. The majestic creatures invoked by its Noongar names – *Dwerda Weelardinup*, meaning 'Place of Dingo Spirit' and *Walyalup* or 'Sea Eagle's nest' – are, however, nowhere in evidence to our always out-of-place eyes.

Week 8, Day 7

We clamber up to the look-out, where Fremantle harbour spreads before us. Where British armies once watched for submarines (invasion anxieties beset this settler nation) our apprehensive gaze is focused on the *Artania,* looking deceptively shipshape as it lies under quarantine. Interrupting the hush we now take for granted, there are helicopters flying overhead. Like the more notorious *Diamond Princess* and *Ruby Princess*, the *Artania* is a floating paradox: a cruise ship devoted to luxury and indulgence now turned into an object of fear and abjection, an incubator of virus.

The *Artania* docked in Fremantle under circumstances for which the cruise operator, the state government and the federal government all disavow responsibility. Eighty-one people were diagnosed with COVID-19 and taken onshore to hospital and quarantine, leading to three fatalities, one a member of the crew. Hundreds more crew and passengers remain on board. Along with that of the *Ruby Princess*, linked to the country's largest outbreak of over 800 infections, the presence of the *Artania* transfixes Australia for weeks. Perhaps one reason is that the cruise ship, indeed, feels like a chronotope of this COVID-19 moment. In the shape of these gleaming hulks, time thickens, takes on flesh. These opulent unmoored containers of disease encapsulate the most violent contradictions of globalization – its environmental ravages, its travesties of luxury for the aspirational classes and surplus populations of capitalist excess, its stark racialized inequalities covered over by a veneer of multicultural geniality between crew and passengers. Before our eyes, they turn into artefacts of a bygone era, like wrecks preserved at the bottom of the ocean, engulfed by unknown but instantaneous catastrophe.

In the spectacle of the cruise ships, too, echoes of this country's recent and not-so-recent past: maritime arrivals from whom we turn away our faces, fortress states, prison islands. Eighteen miles offshore lies the island of Wadjemup, where Rottnest Prison was established just a few years after Captain Charles Fremantle hoisted the British flag at the mouth of the Derbarl Yerrigan in 1829, and claimed this coast for George IV. Aboriginal prisoners were ferried to Rottnest Prison in neck chains and shackles. At night families would signal to their imprisoned kin on Wadjemup through secret fires on Cantonment Hill. Hundreds of them would never see their homelands again.

Week 9, Day 1

Since those days, as a nation we have become adept at offshore detention. Locked up in a hotel in Melbourne for over a year, 60 men brought to the mainland for medical treatment after seven years on Manus Island. They appeal for help: 'it's like a cruise ship in here ... The problem is that they have brought the virus inside this place' (Baker, 2020). Indeed, private security operators alternate between the outsourced detention of refugees and the outsourced detention of quarantined travellers. Disturbing patterns link the quarantine of travellers and the detention of asylum seekers and refugees.

An account yet remains to be written of the ways in which the virus redraws borders and blurs edges between groups while, at the same time, through violence against refugee and migrant bodies, political and epidemiological borders reinforce one another. The *New York Times* (2020) editorializes that through its deportations of migrants the US is 'consciously spreading the pandemic beyond its borders ... to poor countries ill equipped to cope with the disease'. In Australia, international students become trapped in ways that remind us of asylum seekers, deprived of the means of life to stay, yet unable to leave.

This pandemic makes borders legible in new ways. For some, the death counts and interactive maps tracking the global movement of the virus recall the monitoring of sea journeys and charting of refugee movements. For others, the act of crossing borders is made visible anew, as different sorts of bodies are ensnared at airports and surveillance points. These redraw once again the permeable lines between rights and rightlessness, the privileges and limits of citizenship. Different biopolitical permutations are playing out before our eyes from moment to moment:

> Covid-19 is teaching many of us what it feels like to be dislocated from the past and face a future that hangs in the balance, to scan the faces of loved ones on grainy video calls for signs of illness or worry, to have our travel documents become meaningless, to feel unable to seek healthcare, to wonder who will be taken from us before we all land somewhere safe. Yet most of us are facing

this discontinuity in our homes, speaking of the return to 'normality' as a place of refuge and belonging. There's a port at the end of all this. (Shahvisi, 2020)

When the 'second wave' broke in Melbourne, officials were quick to justify the hard lockdown imposed without warning on the Housing Commission towers, home mostly to refugee communities. Drawing on now entrenched associations of blameworthiness, the towers are described as 'vertical cruise ships'. The irony of comparing the affluent lifestyles associated with the *Artania* or *Ruby Princess* to the run-down and unsafe accommodation provided for the state's most disadvantaged seemed lost on many. It was left to Ahmed Dini, a resident of the towers, to point out the stark realities of racialized deprivation and denial of rights experienced by those living in the towers: 'To use the word detention for Australian citizens ... most of these people might as well be stuck on Manus Island' (ABC Radio National, 2020).[2]

Daniel Reeders (2020), whose experience in public health dates back to the Aids crisis, pointed out that

> the outbreak emerged out of clusters among casualized workers in meat works, aged care, childcare, private security, fast food and freight [where] the workers are often employed by labour hire firms and 'booked' shift by shift ... Many are temporary migrants and ... losing a job can mean instant family hardship.

This casual-yet-essential racialized workforce keeps the abattoirs and aged care functioning – and keeps the cruise ships in business.

Week 12, Day 3

When the *Artania* finally departed Fremantle harbour, under renewed pressure from authorities, locals watched it sail away with mixed feelings. Passengers who were nationals of privileged states had been already removed under special dispensation to be flown home on chartered flights. Those remaining on board were mostly crew, sailing into the unknown. School kids who had written postcards to these stranded seafarers throughout the weeks of stand-off were there to wave them off. The moment of departure was almost festive as, in a gallant gesture, two crew members got married a few metres from the gangplank shortly before embarking. Months later, according to CNN, over 50,000 crew members remain on board empty cruise ships, adrift on various oceans. Seafarers, an invisible population and a new type of globalization's castaways.

Week 13, Day 4

Imperceptibly, the weeks have moved on. Looking out on another type of carrier from the crest of Cantonment Hill, we are aware of the chilly squalls of Makuru. All day, the wind from the docks has set us on edge, the dogs unusually alert, the humans decidedly queasy. The stench is all too familiar in this port city: thousands of sheep, trucked to the docks for loading on to ships for the long voyage north. Many of us have stories of terrified sheep and cattle, desperate to escape, making a dive for freedom. Some manage to swim to shore, or are rescued, lowing for help, only to be taken back on board. A few years ago, a cow leapt overboard and managed to swim to the beach. She ran desperately along the foreshore eluding pursuit, before collapsing of a heart attack in full view of beach goers. In the face of these everyday local cruelties, most of us know how to avert our eyes and hold our noses.

Sheep and cows are intertwined with settler Australia's story: to make way for sheep, Indigenous people and their animals, especially the dingo, were displaced, and at times actively eliminated (Mayes, 2020). Attacks on sheep were understood as an existential threat to the settler ethos and Indigenous men were executed for the offence of sheep-stealing, or else taken to Rottnest jail in chains. Shearers, stockmen and graziers, on the other hand, enjoy mythic status as a type of national hero. It is a truism that Australia's post-World War 2 prosperity is 'built on the sheep's back'.

Today we woke to the news that the spread of COVID-19 among the crew of a sheep transport vessel has thrown a spanner in the works of the live export trade. The *Al Kuwait*, which was berthed adjacent to the *Artania*, now has a number of infected crew and is unable to set sail. Fifty-six thousand sheep, brought to the docks in stinking trucks yesterday, are now loaded up again and taken to a feed-lot to await the outcome of a ruling on whether the ship can sail with a new crew. A ban is in place on sheep carriers departing after 1 June, directly into the heat of the northern summer. It was put in place after horrific revelations in 2018 of sheep subjected to conditions of extreme heat on transport ships.

Week 15, Day 2

The exporters sought an exception to the ruling to allow the *Al Kuwait* to sail regardless. It dragged on for nearly three weeks. Eventually, despite the risk to the sheep from heightened temperatures due to an 18-day delay in setting out, the ship was cleared to leave. Before a court injunction could be sought to stop it, the *Al Kuwait* sailed out of Fremantle harbour with 50,000 sheep on board.

From the Place of Dingo Spirit, we look down on the purpose-built sheep carrier *Al Kuwait*. Unlike in the case of the *Artania*, few of us, except for a handful of determined protesters, had the heart to watch it depart.

Week 15, Day 6

Pandemic temporality combines an intense stasis, a sense of having lost track of days and weeks, with a frantic attention to the moment; our hyperactive online lives obsessively track media across multiple news cycles. As we monitor infection trends and compare death counts from the stillness of lockdown, times of lag and times of escalation merge. At other times, online life overruns the space of our lockdown lives, collapsing the categories and frameworks that hold each in place. The killing of George Floyd is one such instance. Abruptly, the accustomed tempo of everyday life in viral times collides with the insistent presence of what Alexandra Juhasz named – in 2016, when virality was only a convenient metaphor – *viral black death*: the circulation of video and webcam footage witnessing the public killing of Black Americans by agents of the state (Juhasz, 2016; Fain, 2016).

George Floyd was murdered in plain sight by Derek Chauvin and fellow members of the Minneapolis Police Department. What made this footage so distinctive among the proliferation of citizen-recorded police killings, Ava DuVernay (2020) remarks in the immediate aftermath, is that the faces of both victim and killer are simultaneously before us, 'perfectly framed' by the camera during the long minutes of the killing. Both the prone, suffocating face of George Floyd and the calculatedly nonchalant countenance of his killer are caught for the viewer in a shattering symmetry. We look them both in the eye. This perhaps accounts for how this ultimate artefact of viral black death resounds in profound and global ways with the virality of the times.

Week 16, Day 4

George Floyd was killed by Derek Chauvin and fellow police officers, but the autopsy reveals that Floyd was by then already infected with COVID-19. Both George Floyd and Breona Taylor, his fellow-victim of police killing who nursed those hospitalized by the virus, are part of what Steven W. Thrasher names the viral underclass: 'a population harmed not simply by microscopic organisms but by the societal structures that make viral transmission possible': that is, structures of racialized disposability and economic precarity (Thrasher, 2020).

The killing of George Floyd thus was a moment of deep clarification, a making visible, across the globe, of the ways in which we experience 'the societal structures that make viral transmission possible' on so many levels of daily life. '*I can't breathe,*' the desperate last words of George Floyd and Eric Garner as US police stifled their lives out of them, were repeated 12 times by the young Dunghutti man, David Dungay, suffocated to death by five prison officials in Sydney's Long Bay gaol in 2016 (Pugliese, 2018).

As a call to action by Black Lives Matter protesters, in Australia as in the US, *I can't breathe* refers to suffocation within the monumentality of white racial 'societal structures', symbolic and material.

Week 17, Day 3

The protests that followed the killings of George Floyd and Breona Taylor, first in the US and then in other global cities, also clarified that the logic of Black Lives Matter is a localized and spatial logic: the logic of everyday lives lived in nominated topographies, delineated in the names of public spaces, our squares, parks and streets, and shaped in the seemingly enduring shadow of monuments of racial power. The built environments of US cities, their highways and skyscrapers, stand as monuments to the same forces that erected statues of confederate generals.

Following the toppling of statues of slave traders and imperial murderers in Europe, the state government of Western Australia quickly announced that the King Leopold Ranges, more than 2,000 kilometres away from the state capital, from now are to be known officially as the Wunaamin-Miliwundi Ranges, following consultation with local groups. The Ranges were renamed from their original Ngarinyin and Bunuba names in 1879 by Alexander Forrest, described as an explorer, surveyor and land agent – trades indistinguishable from the appropriation and dispossession of Aboriginal country. His brother, also a land agent and surveyor, went on to become the state's first Premier. Today, the Forrest family is associated with a vast network of mining, trade, financial and philanthropic interests, all buttressed by immense wealth, land holdings and political influence (Mitchell, 2019).

Like the names of other powerful settler families – Canning, Stirling, Roe – that shape our built environment and the very infrastructure of the state, the name Forrest appears on many street signs, highways, buildings and statues. Aboriginal families who bear the same names signal ties of patronage or blood to these powerful men, forged in the crucible of violent settler histories. No official moves are announced to reconsider the ubiquitous memorialization of these names. They remain part of the monumental infrastructure of settler violence, naturalized, largely invisible.

Week 17, Day 5

As Black Lives Matter protests spread across Australian cities, Prime Minister Scott Morrison casts them as an irrelevant distraction. In Australia, he says, 'there was no slavery' (Borys, 2020). (Later, he would retract this statement.)

The day after Morrison's remarks, we are gathered once again in the shadow of Cantonment Hill, at sunset, on a site looking out to Fremantle harbour. The Derbarl Yerrigan spreads below us. Off in the distance, out of view but an enduring presence, is the prison island of Rottnest.

We stand before a local landmark, a sculpture known as Rainbow, by artist Marcus Canning. The site, Number 1 Canning Highway, is at a local crossroads, with Stirling Bridge across the water. The sculpture, a series of multicoloured shipping containers linked into the shape of an arch, invokes the inclusive openness of a port city, a gateway to all that lies beyond. It is a monument to rainbow optimism that puts our best face forward. Usually, it is a spot much favoured by tourists. Today, there are none to be seen, just a small, socially distanced group of locals. Motorists pass by on Canning Highway, sound an occasional sympathetic honk.

Hannah McGlade, Noongar activist, academic, speaks, directly addressing the prime minister's claims that there was no slavery in Australia:

> Across the world, people are making a powerful stand against racial oppression, violence and inequality that is rendering Black lives very unsafe.
>
> Since 1990 more than 434 Aboriginal people have died in police and prison custody. Since George Floyd was killed in Minneapolis by an officer now charged with murder, we have here in Perth witnessed the death of an Aboriginal man at Acacia prison, and an Aboriginal woman at Bandyup is in critical condition after being body-slammed by guards …
>
> The Prime Minister thinks that Black Lives Matter should not be imported into this country from overseas. He said we had no slavery in this country.
>
> The first building erected in the Swan River Colony was the Roundhouse in Fremantle, it was built in 1830 to incarcerate Aboriginal men who resisted colonists' attempts to enslave and indenture them to wealthy pastoralists. Many of the men forcibly taken in neck chains to Rottnest, Wadjemup, died at the island, many were executed and this island is the largest mass grave in Australia today.
>
> I am the great-granddaughter of Ethel Woyung who was indentured as a girl and whose brother Mindum was incarcerated at Wadjemup which he escaped …
>
> When we say Black Lives matter, here in Australia, we are speaking of Ms Dhu, Cherdeena Wynne, Chad Riley, Joyce Clarke, and many more.
>
> We remember the two young men who died after being chased into the Derbarl Yerrigan river on a cold and windy day by police.

And we remember our people once pursued on order of Governor Stirling and chased into the Murray River (Pinjarra River) and shot at. They were massacred, men, women and children. …

They told us not to come [today]. They told us to be silent.

We will not be silent. We will say their names. (McGlade, 2020)

As McGlade speaks, the ghost of Alfred Canning, for whom this highway is named, is not far away. Canning is another architect of the settler infrastructure of this state. His projects include the Rabbit Proof Fence and the Canning Stock Route, designed to open beef markets for the graziers of the north. Following his work on the stock route, Canning faced a Royal Commission of inquiry on charges relating to his treatment of the Indigenous people in its path. They included:

Forcing the natives to accompany the party; Chaining by the neck natives who had done nothing to deserve being deprived of their liberty …; Unnecessarily depriving natives of their water supply by deepening and squaring their native wells rendering it impossible for old men, women and … [children] to reach the water; and causing the water to be polluted by animals falling in; Hunting native women on foot and horseback, sometimes with rifles, for immoral purposes; Using threats and giving bribes to native men to induce them to direct their women to have connection with the members of the expedition. (National Museum of Australia, 2016)

Canning was acquitted on all charges.

On this site at 1 Canning Highway, in the shadow of Cantonment Hill, overlooking the Derbarl Yerrigan and extending out to the harbour, we have decided to project the

Figure 9.1: Saying Their Names, Walyalup/Fremantle 2020

names of some of the hundreds of Indigenous people who died in custody on the Rainbow sculpture by Marcus Canning.

The last of the Makuru sun inflames the arc with a fiery intensity before subsiding into a steady half-light. The names keep coming: *Lloyd Boney. Christine Jones. Ms Dhu. Alfred Dougal, David Gundy. David Dungay. Cherdeena Wynne. Chad Riley, Mr Ward.* And so many more.

Week 18, Day 1

The small family with their camp tucked out of sight of Canning Highway, looking out on the Derbarl Yerrigan, has moved on overnight, a sign that the lockdown is starting to ease here on the west coast. Soon, the rhythm of our walks will become more desultory, less weighted, integrated back into the business of everyday living. Viral lives, viral deaths. This virus, for so many of us, has acted as a clarifier of the histories, places and environments in which we live. How else to explain the nightly protests that continue months later, in so many US cities, and elsewhere? In this small Indian Ocean town, the turns and returns of my virus walk-story retrace a terrain that is both already known and brought newly into view: our lives in the viral times of COVID-19 are not to be separated from the viral deaths of George Floyd and the many other deaths that come before and after.

We look them in the eye.

Fremantle/Walyalup
March–July 2020

Notes

1   A longer version of this piece was published in the journal *Overland* in February 2021.
2   Refugees and those who seek asylum by boat are held in offshore detention camps in Manus Island, Papua New Guinea, by the Australian government.

References

Baker, N. (2020) '"It's like a cruise ship in here": Asylum seekers 'terrified' after COVID-19 infection in Melbourne detention hotel', *SBS News*, 14 July. www.sbs.com.au/news/it-s-like-a-cru ise-ship-in-here-asylum-seekers-terrified-after-covid-19-infect ion-in-melbourne-detention-hotel

Borys, S. (2020) 'Prime minister criticised after suggesting 'no slavery' in Australia's history', *ABC Radio*, PM with Linda Mottram, 11 June. www.abc.net.au/radio/programs/pm/prime-minister-cri ticised-after-suggesting-no-slavery/12346388

de Certeau, M. (1994 [1998]) *The Practice of Everyday Life*, Vol. 2, translated by T.J. Tomasik, University of Minnesota Press.

Dini, A. (2020) 'Melbourne housing commission residents forced into lockdown', *ABC Radio*, RN Breakfast with Patricia Karvelas, 6 July. www.abc.net.au/radionational/programs/breakfast/ melbourne-housing-commission-residents-forced-into-lockd own/12424530

DuVernay, A. (2020) Interview on The Ellen Show, 8 June. www. youtube.com/watch?v=vrYaj-Wi0o8

Fain, K. (2016) 'Viral black death: why we must watch citizen videos of police violence', *JSTOR Daily*, 1 September. https://daily.jstor. org/why-we-must-watch-citizen-videos-of-police-violence/

Juhasz, A. (2016) 'How do I (not) look? Live feed video and viral black death', *JSTOR Daily*, 20 July. https://daily.jstor.org/ how-do-i-not-look/

Mayes, C. (2020) 'Governmentality of fencing in Australia: tracing the white wires from paddocks to Aboriginal protection, pest exclusion and immigration restriction', *Journal of Intercultural Studies*, 41(1): 42–59.

McGlade, H. (2020) 'Kaya Nidja Noongar Boodjah', speech at Perth Black Lives Matter Protest, National Indigenous TV, 17 June. www.sbs.com.au/nitv/article/2020/06/17/kaya-nidja-noon gar-boodjah-perth-black-lives-matter-rally-2020?fbclid=IwAR 1ZLd5YzuNaBkVPR9Ivyy8X8tJT7WUnPBvWRmJ0VTTM v42RgcSPu5_R8RY

Mitchell, R. (2019) 'How WA's first premier Sir John Forrest, brother Alexander Forrest built this State', *The West Australian*, 6 May. https://thewest.com.au/news/wa/how-was-first-premier-sir-john-forrest-brother-alexander-forrest-built-this-state-ng-b881184593z

National Museum of Australia (2016) The Legacy of Alfred Canning. www.nma.gov.au/__data/assets/pdf_file/0016/19411/Yiwarra-Kuju-Alfred-Canning.pdf

New York Times (2020) 'Why is the United States exporting coronavirus?', 18 June.

Pugliese, J. (2018) 'A series of daily dispatches from the coronial inquest currently underway in Sydney for Mr David Dungay, Dunghutti Warrior', *Deathscapes*. www.deathscapes.org/engagements/dispatch-sydney/

Reeders, D. (2020) 'Weapons of mask distraction', *Inside Story*, 22 July. https://insidestory.org.au/weapons-of-mask-distraction/

Shahvisi, A. (2020) 'Counting Deaths', *London Review of Books* blog, 17 April. www.lrb.co.uk/blog/2020/april/counting-deaths

Thrasher, S.W (2020). 'An Uprising Comes From the Viral Underclass' (2020), *Slate*, 12 June. www.slate.com/news-and-politics/2020/06/black-lives-matter-viral-underclass.html (accessed 13 July 2020).

TEN

The Virus and the Violence: Reflections on 'Anti-Asian' Hate and Racist Maskaphobia[1]

Mengzhu Fu

Introduction

Since the beginning of the COVID-19 pandemic, we have witnessed a transnational surge in 'anti-Asian' violence. These 'incidents' of violence have often involved what Yixuan Huang calls 'maskaphobia' coupled with 'anti-Asian' racism (Young, 2020). The dominant framing of such events has been 'hate crimes', illustrated in the popular hashtag, #StopAsianHate. Drawing on Haritaworn's (2015) argument that 'hate' and 'crime' individualize and pathologize systemic violence, we see that carceral solutions inevitably empower white supremacist systems. From Thobani's (2007) analysis of Canadian citizenship and Lawrence and Dua's (2005) calls for decolonizing anti-racism, we learn that evoking Canadian nationalism as a defence against racism privileges settler colonial modes of belonging. In this chapter, I reflect on how state-based methods to counter racist violence are ineffective and ignore the historical foundations of white supremacy. I analyse the reporting of 'anti-Asian' racism focusing in the Greater Toronto Area (GTA) in conversation with international events and social media discourses. Weaving personal memories, storytelling, histories of anti-Asian racism on Canada-occupied Turtle Island,[2] and academic/activist analysis, I critically reflect on maskaphobia and responses to 'anti-Asian' racism.

First, a note on the imperfect language of 'anti-Asian' racism as a descriptor of COVID-19-related racism that has been commonly framed as 'anti-Asian' hate crimes. While this violence is often targeted at people who 'look Chinese' and uses anti-Chinese rhetoric (Borja et al , 2020), naming this as anti-Chinese racism ignores how this violence impacts beyond Chinese communities. Other East Asians, Southeast Asians and Indigenous peoples who have been mistaken for Asians have all been targets of physical assaults in public spaces (Kong et al, 2021). Calling it anti-Asian racism loses specificity of which Asians (East and Southeast) are targeted and reinforces a Sinocentric tendency that erases West, Central and South Asians who are also 'Asian'. For lack of a better term, I use 'anti-Asian' racism in scare quotes to reference the literature and media that uses this term while denaturalizing it for the nuances I have outlined.

In the first section, I turn to my memories from the start of the pandemic to highlight the connection between maskaphobia and 'anti-Asian' racism. The second section draws attention to the escalations of violence and critiques the discursive and legal framing of acts of public 'anti-Asian' racism as 'hate crimes'. My third section addresses some of the claims to Canadian identity and belonging as a defence against 'anti-Asian' racism and considers how this approach exemplifies a form of complicity in settler colonialism. Instead, 'Asian' anti-racism should be in alignment with Indigenous resurgence and Black abolition in strengthening 'constellations of co-resistance' (Simpson, 2017).

'Anti-Asian' racism during the beginnings of the pandemic

It is December 2019, before news of the coronavirus started circulating in Chinese language media. I am living in Mississauga. It is winter, and freezing cold to my body that has adapted to the milder temperatures of Tāmaki Makaurau, Aotearoa (colonial name: Auckland, New Zealand). I wear a mask gifted by my cousin on my long commutes to and from university, to keep warm. Whenever I visited my extended family in Northern China, I would often wear a mask outside during the winter. The last time I visited, it was Spring, so when we wore masks, it was to filter the toxic smog from the industrial pollution. Even before COVID-19, capitalism and industrial growth attacked lungs in China. These are the situations I remember, of wearing masks to protect myself. At other times, I wear a mask when I am sick, to protect others.

At the beginning of the pandemic, we are in touch with our family in China. My extended family here sends masks over as my family there experience shortages as prices rise. Our primary concern is the health and wellbeing of friends and family in China. Meanwhile, in the news media here, anti-Chinese fearmongering starts, and Orientalist Chinese bat-eating articles are going viral.

It is January 2020. As Chinatowns are now like ghost towns, Chinese communities in Tkaronto are starting to speak out on the growing overt racism (Tsekouras, 2020b). This resurrection of the overt mass-scale Sinophobia echoes the Yellow Peril, the construction of Chinese bodies as contagious and diseased that we saw not long ago during the SARS epidemics of 2003 (Wong, 2020). In the earlier history of Chinese migration to Turtle Island, Shah (2001) has described the demonization and scapegoating of the residents of San Francisco's Chinatown from public health responses during the smallpox epidemic in 1879.

Anti-Chinese and, more broadly, anti-Asian racism, has been a core pillar of Canadian nation-building. Northern Turtle

Island[3] was claimed by white colonizers like John A. Macdonald as a 'white man's country' (Dua, 2007: 446) and renamed 'Canada'. A series of colonial legislation including the head tax was specifically imposed to restrict Chinese immigration. The dangerous labour conditions in the construction of the transcontinental Canadian Pacific Railway made it clear that Chinese people were intended to be temporary and disposable labourers (Yu, 2021). In 1885, the Canadian government restricted Chinese women from immigrating through justifications that associated Chinese women with prostitution (Dua, 2007). These policies also stem from a fear that the Chinese population would reproduce and settle long-term. Fears of miscegenation and threats to white racial purity eventually permitted Chinese, Japanese, and Indian women to immigrate to 'Canada' (Dua, 2007). This history shows that anti-Asian racism is not indigenous to this land but was brought over by European colonizers from their imperialist endeavours in Asia.

It is March 2020. As reports of COVID-19 case numbers start to rise in Toronto, a group of East Asian women is ejected by staff from a supermarket in East Tkaronto. This is after a white woman harassed them *for wearing masks* (Siu, 2020). The white woman is reported to have said: 'You know those masks don't work right? I don't know why you guys have them on but they don't work. Are you wearing it because you have the virus?' (Siu, 2020). This happened before masks became mandatory indoors. By that time, we already knew that asymptomatic people can still spread the virus. If anything, these East Asian women were protecting other shoppers. Instead of acknowledging this as an act of care, racism redefined them as sources of contagion.

April 2020. 'A woman in her 60s' verbally attacks and spits on Katherine Cheung, an emergency room nurse, in downtown Toronto (Tsekouras, 2020a). Cheung says, 'it happened because I'm Asian and wearing a mask' (Tsekouras, 2020b). Stories of 'Asian' women being punched and assaulted in the streets while wearing masks are common by now (Young, 2020). This violence is gendered, and 'Asian' health care workers are experiencing this while working at the frontlines of the pandemic.

May 2020. A white man refusing to wear a mask indoors in an Asian grocery store in Mississauga verbally and racially abuses an elder East Asian grocery worker (Yeung, 2020). When staff ask the white man to leave, he bursts into a racist tirade: "This is a communist virus from China, from you guys." He repeatedly yells the question, "where are you from?" in close range to the staff, to which a worker responds, "we are Canadian". The worker repeats, "I am Canadian" as the white man ridicules his claim to Canadianness. The racial insults and the misinformation about masks continue until workers finally make him leave the store. By then, for many East Asians, staying indoors meant sheltering from both the virus and the violence.

Understanding maskaphobia

These early pandemic examples of public 'anti–Asian' racism have in common the mask as the central object of contention. While doing research for Dr Jin Haritaworn, I came across the term 'maskaphobia', coined by Dr Yinxuan Huang to name this new iteration of racism specific to the pandemic (Young, 2020). Maskaphobia has been defined as 'discrimination and racism against people wearing face masks' (Young, 2020). The link between pandemic 'anti–Asian' racism and maskaphobia has been documented in the US (Leung, 2020) and Canada (Tsekouras, 2020a). Huang (quoted in Young, 2020) explains maskaphobia as a 'cultural difference' between East and West mask-wearing practices and meanings, a view that other journalists, too, have foregrounded. Ansari (2020) argues that individualism in North America plays a role in responses to masks, which are seen as a symbol that evokes fear and panic rather than a symbol of solidarity. Masks have been associated with criminality and political extremism, which goes back to the history of anti-mask laws in the US and Canada (Ansari, 2020). While indebted to Yinxuan Huang's conceptual work, attending to the history of masking as a public health measure challenges cultural essentialist explanations.

The beginning of mask use as a public health response was developed by Dr Wu Lien-teh in order to prevent the spread of the pneumonic plague in 1910 (Howard et al, 2021). In the 99% Invisible (2020) podcast episode 'Masking for a Friend', Vivian Huang states: 'It's really taken Chinese people 100 years to get to this point of acceptance of wearing masks during an infectious disease outbreak. And now it's to the point where people would just wear them when they've got a cold.'

Huang further explains that masks in China were mandated as part of the state's public health policy and became a symbol of medical success to prevent disease (99% Invisible, 2020).

From the start of the COVID-19 pandemic, the combination of masks and yellow skin became a target for white supremacists who were quick to blame the pandemic on all Chinese people. In the media, this association was aided by the rapid circulation of images of mask-wearing East Asians alongside news about the spread of coronavirus. These visual framings accompanied a discursive slide between 'Asians', masks, and coronavirus that likely contributed to a rise in 'anti-Asian' racism transnationally (Batova, 2021.

Escalations of 'anti-Asian' violence in 2021

A year into the COVID-19 pandemic, 'anti-Asian' and other forms of racist violence have only escalated. On Canada-occupied Turtle Island, there was an 800 per cent increase in 'anti-Asian' racist violence. The Chinese-Canadian National Council Toronto Chapter released a report based on data collected between 10 March 2020 and 28 February 2021. In that time, there were 1,150 reports of racist attacks across Canada-occupied Turtle Island (Kong et al, 2021). In their executive summary of statistics of 'anti-Asian' racist incidents, they note that 60 per cent of reports came from Asian women, 84 per cent of reports were from East Asians and 6 per cent from Southeast Asians. Reports were also made by those who identified themselves as biracial, Indigenous, South Asian, Black and Central Asian. Among other statistics, the report found Asian frontline and essential workers are more vulnerable to racial attacks. Those who reported in Chinese were twice as likely to experience physical assault than those who reported in English (Kong et al, 2021: 6).

February 2021, we see the violent attacks and murders of East and Southeast Asian elders in US-occupied Turtle Island (Bote, 2021). April 2021, the news of a mass shooting targeting Asian massage workers in Atlanta, Georgia, devastates Asian communities across the world (Cho 2021). 'Anti-Asian' racism is gendered and gendered violence is racialized. As Elene Lam of Butterfly, an Asian and migrant sex worker support network in Tkaronto, emphasizes, intersectionality is needed in our approaches to 'anti-Asian' racism, along with acknowledging that the violence in Atlanta is underscored by whorephobia (Sukhdeo, 2021). Organizations representing Asian and migrant sex workers such as Red Canary Song in New York and Butterfly (Sukhdeo, 2021) in Toronto have explicitly opposed increased policing as a response to the harm against migrant massage parlour and sex workers.

'Anti-Asian' violence cannot be reduced to an emotion

Several initiatives have emerged across North America to document and collect data on 'anti-Asian' violence, from campaigns such as Stop AAPI Hate to the social media hashtag #StopAsianHate. Incidents of 'anti-Asian' physical violence from strangers have been described in the news as 'hate crimes' that are often followed by police investigations (Fox, 2020). In Haritaworn's (2015) critique of hate/crime paradigms, they argue that hate 'has the same individualising, depoliticising tendencies as neoliberal discourses overall' (Haritaworn, 2015: 140). In their abolitionist analysis of queer hate crime activism in Berlin, the impulsive 'hateful Other' is racialized and Muslim, love is then a noble affect reserved for the white queers who are worthy of the state's protection. With #StopAsianHate, the adjective before 'hate' is 'Asian' instead of 'white' despite the perpetrators being overwhelmingly white (Yam, 2021). Whiteness is elided in the naming of the problem and in associations with 'hate' (Yu, 2021).

In the UK, Kay (2020) highlights a pattern where anti-Black and Muslim 'hate crime' incidents are taken less seriously. On Turtle Island too, racially motivated 'hate crimes' seem to be primarily used in incidents of anti-East Asian racist violence. When Black and Indigenous peoples are targeted or when the police are the perpetrators, 'hate crime' is not the dominant interpretation. The visibility of 'hate crimes' furthermore overshadows the daily structural racism of border imperialism (Walia, 2013), the policing and harassment of Asian and migrant sex workers (Sukhdeo, 2021), and the lack of accountability for anti-Black and anti-Indigenous murders committed by or involving police. If 'hate crime' recognized the state's racist violence, the colonial police forces would be visible as the most organized and well-resourced hate criminals. This pattern where 'anti-Asian' violence is interpreted as 'hate crimes' reflects who is worthy of protection from the state and for whom state violence is the norm. Instead of 'hate crime' where the state becomes the provider of protection, we should treat 'anti-Asian' racism as embedded in the formation of the Canadian state, as part of a history that is entangled with deep-seated anti-Blackness (Sharpe, 2016; Maynard, 2017) and ongoing settler colonization (Simpson, 2017). This racism is made more visible in interpersonal public acts of violence during the pandemic but has consistently been there in the white supremacist infrastructures of the Canadian state, its institutions and economy.

Refusing Canadian nationalism

My heart breaks remembering the Asian elder in the Mississauga grocery store who repeated "I am Canadian" as a shield against a white man's racist verbal abuse (Yeung, 2020). It didn't protect him, and it won't protect any of us. The tactic to gain acceptance through 'Canadian' identity has clearly failed. In efforts to fight 'anti-Asian' xenophobia, these kinds of appeals to settler colonial national belonging are perhaps elicited to gain empathy or respect, but respect and safety should not be contingent on affiliation with Canadian identity.

March 2021, I am attending a rally against 'anti-Asian' racism in Toronto. I am thankful to the organizers for creating this space for collective healing, grief and power. Many of the speakers and statements contextualize 'anti-Asian' racism in Canadian histories of racist discrimination and white supremacy, and express solidarity with Indigenous, Black, and Muslim communities. Thankfully, this rally does not have a pro-policing stance, but it is not without displays of Canadian nationalism. As I scan the crowd, I notice a few Canadian flags. One of the speeches ends with a declaration of 'We are Canadians!' We learn from Indigenous scholars and activists on Turtle Island that Canadian statecraft continues to rely on dispossession, genocide and extraction from unceded Indigenous territories (Lawrence and Dua, 2005; Simpson, 2017). This reach for Canadian national belonging and inclusion into Canadian citizenship reflects 'Asian' complicity in settler colonialism (Thobani, 2007). Chen (2021) observes similar issues at a 'Stop Asian Hate' rally in Vancouver: 'The fetishistic faith in the Canadian flag, a symbol of white supremacy, settler-colonialism, and imperialism, as a shield to repel racism is at best ineffectual and at worst a bid by middle class and bourgeois Chinese-Canadians to win a seat at the genocidal table alongside white settlers.'

In contrast, alignment with Indigenous resistance to colonialism would involve, as Lawrence (2003: 5) articulated, 'a refusal to accept the authority of Canada or the United States as settler states'. Furthermore, for non-Canadian Chinese like myself, the 'we are Canadians' response inadvertently implies that those who are not Canadian do not deserve the same safety. This illustrates Thobani's critique of exaltation as a process that 'constitutes the national subject as belonging to a higher order of humanity' and thus Canadians are 'intrinsically deserving of greater rights and entitlements' (2007: 248). Following Indigenous calls to #CancelCanadaDay (Idle No More, 2021), if we cancel Canadian nationalism, we might move towards closer alignment with Indigenous resurgence.

Conclusion

In this chapter, I have explored how 'anti-Asian' violence during this pandemic has relied on racist maskaphobia, which reinterprets acts of care as symbols of contagion. In these times of crisis, Haritaworn (2020: 5) has argued, 'Our masks are defiant fashion symbols, of ethnic pride and genius, of solidarity.' Throughout the pandemic, we wear masks at each other's protests, we wear masks proudly to protect each other, in recognition that our health is interdependent, and that our liberation is intertwined.

By critiquing the paradigm of 'hate/crime', I do not want to diminish the impact of individual acts of violence: the rise in 'anti-Asian' violence has devastated communities around the world while living through a pandemic. I am interested in long-term solutions that do not rely on the state as a source of safety. Explaining 'anti-Asian' violence through the prism of hate stops short of addressing the histories of anti-Asian and structural violence. The pandemic and the associated 'anti-Asian' racism have not only had physical and emotional impacts, but also educational (Balingit et al, 2021) and economic effects (Madan et al, 2021), which become eclipsed by the sensationalism of the label 'hate crimes'. These consequences are not only based on hate, they are also about power and extraction of land, labour and resources. Interpreting these acts of violence as isolated individual incidents, stemming from feelings of 'hate', reduces 'anti-Asian' racism to an emotion devoid of political context (Haritaworn, 2015).

If hate is not the problem, then 'love', alone, is not the solution. Citing Dr Martin Luther King Jr, Dr Moana Jackson (2019), has articulated: '[W]hile love might prompt a desire for change, the change itself could not occur without the practical exertion 'of weary feet and sharp minds'. It involved active toil and an honest analysis of historic cause and consequence, as well as the willingness to dream different dreams.'

In dreaming 'different dreams', we might dream of abolition, of futures where police and prisons become obsolete (Davis, 2016), where Indigenous nations regain full sovereignty over their land and waters. We might dream of abundance and economies outside of capitalist extractivism. Of relationalities founded on mutual aid (Haritaworn, 2020; Madan et al, 2021), solidarity, and 'constellations of co-resistance' (Simpson, 2017).

These relationalities are already in prefigurative practice before and during the pandemic. In February 2021, Sam Wong (Métis/Chinese) from Indigenous youth-led organization, Assembly of Seven Generations (2021), hosted an online conversation on 'Building Better Relations' between Chinese and Indigenous communities focusing on addressing anti-Chinese and anti-Indigenous racism, and ageism. In a live-translated bilingual (Mandarin/English) conversation, Gabrielle Fayant (Métis), co-founder of Assembly of Seven Generations started off by acknowledging the longstanding relationships Indigenous and Chinese people have had since the late 1800s and even before that, where a lot of her relations 'would almost seek refuge with Chinese businesses because we weren't allowed to go into white businesses or even white towns at times'. In Mandarin, Chinese elders from Yet Keen told stories about the origins and traditions of Spring Festival (lunar new year), exchanging cultural knowledge with Indigenous youth and elders. In December 2021, the Chinese Canadian National

Council – Toronto and the Yarrow Society (2021) organized workshops on colonialism and Indigenous histories featuring Indigenous land defender, Kwitsel Tatel (Sto:lo), speaking on her experiences with police violence and the colonial court system. She invited 'Asian relatives' to take action to defund the police and defend Indigenous rights to water and land because 'decolonizing takes teamwork'.

As we adapt to new phases of the pandemic, these instances of story-sharing, of direct inter-community and intergenerational relationship-building are ever more potent for growing underground mycelium networks. May we draw strength from each other and the soil to bring these 'different dreams' to fruition.

Notes

1   This article is part of a SSHRC-funded research project led by Dr Jin Haritaworn on 'Subversive Performances of Quarantine: Organizing Across Differences at the Conjuncture of Protest and the Pandemic'. Much gratitude and appreciation for Dr Jin Haritaworn, Dr Arama Rata, Dr Sunera Thobani and Dr Mahdis Azarmandi for providing thoughtful feedback and edits on previous drafts.

2   A name for North America used by many Indigenous peoples.

3   Influenced by Linda Tuhiwai Smith's (1999) work on the politics of (re)naming as a colonizing practice, I use northern Turtle Island to respectfully refer to these lands as Indigenous peoples have named them and to distinguish it from US-occupied Turtle Island. Curtis Clearsky of Blackfoot and Anishinaabe First Nations in 2012 referred to so-called Canada as 'northern Turtle Island' in *Our Roots: Stories from Grandview Woodland*, Vancouver Dialogues. 'Canada' is used to refer to the colonial nation state structures as illegitimate occupying powers.

References

99% Invisible (2020) 'Masking for a Friend', podcast. https:// podcastaddict.com/episode/102816136?fbclid=IwAR2Mt6KSJ 1VXMQPDSiSupJR1E4htnP0k2XBXBMLY3SlQh4O9N84h n6DBXF4

Ansari, S. (2020) 'The history of our cultural resistance against masks', *Maclean's*, 22 April. www.macleans.ca/opinion/the-hist ory-of-our-cultural-resistance-against-masks/

Assembly of Seven Generations (2021) 'Building Better Relations Webinar Series: Chinese New Year', *YouTube*. www.youtube. com/watch?v=3s4M8g-9zhI

Balingit, M., Natanson, H. and Chen, Y. (2021) 'As schools reopen, Asian American students are missing from classrooms', *The Seattle Times*, 4 March. www.seattletimes.com/nation-world/as-schools-reopen-asian-american-students-are-missing-from-classrooms/ ?fbclid=IwAR3wooBZUfKRfA8lLrm7s5M9wBeNeRoCBTifn iXUo9zA-kjZTfKiRTEDGcE

Batova, T. (2021) '"Picturing" Xenophobia: Visual Framing of Masks During COVID-19 and Its Implications for Advocacy in Technical Communication', *Journal of Business and Technical Communication*, 35(1): 50–56.

Borja, M., Jeung, R., Yellow Horse, A., Gibson, J., Gowing, S., Lin, N., Navins, A. and Power, E. (2020) Anti-Chinese rhetoric tied to racism against Asian Americans: Stop AAPI Hate Report. https://stopaapihate.org/wp-content/uploads/2021/04/Stop-AAPI-Hate-Report-Anti-China-Rhetoric-200617.pdf

Bote, J. (2021) 'An elderly San Francisco man was killed in a "brutal" attack. His family says it was a racist act', *SFGATE*, 2 February. www.sfgate.com/crime/article/elderly-San-Francisco-man-kil led-racist-act-Vicha-15918274.php

Chen, L. (2021) 'Doubling down on Canadian nationalism won't end anti-Asian hate', *The Volcano*, 31 March. http://thevolcano.org/ 2021/03/31/canadian-nationalism-wont-end-anti-asian-hate/

Chinese Canadian National Council Toronto and Yarrow Society (2021) 'Workshop #1: Colonialism and Indigenous History'. www.instagram.com/p/CXMjnPgvQ-t/

Cho, D.J. (2021) 'Moving moments from Stop Asian Hate rallies that have taken place around the world', *People*, 6 April. https:// people.com/human-interest/stop-asian-hate-protest-photos/?

Clearsky, C. (n.d.) *In Our Roots: Stories from Grandview-Woodland*. Social Policy. https://vancouverdialoguesandyouthvry.files.wordpress.com/2012/09/dialogues-project-our-roots-stories-from-grandview-woodland-final-book.pdf

Davis, A.Y. (2016) *Freedom is a Constant Struggle: Ferguson, Palestine, and the Foundations of a Movement*. Haymarket Books.

Dua, E. (2007) 'Exclusion through inclusion: Female Asian migration in the making of Canada as a white settler nation', *Gender, Place & Culture*, 14(4): 445–66.

Fox, C. (2020) 'Police charge man in connection with racist, anti-mask rant at Mississauga supermarket', *CTV News*, 16 July. https://toronto.ctvnews.ca/police-charge-man-in-connection-with-racist-anti-mask-rant-at-mississauga-supermarket-1.5026907

Haritaworn, J. (2015) *Queer Lovers and Hateful Others: Regenerating Violent Times and Places*. Pluto.

Haritaworn, J. (2020) '# NoGoingBack: Queer leaps at the intersection of protest and COVID-19', *Journal of Environmental Media*, 1(2): 12–1.

Howard, J., Huant, A., Li, Z., Tufekci, Z., Zdimal, V., van der Westhuizen, H.-M., von Delft, A., Price, A., Fridman, L., Tang, L.-H., Tang, V., Watson, G.L., Bax, C.E., Shaikh, R., Questier, F., Hernandez, D., Chu, L.F., Ramirez, C.M. and Rimoin, A.W. (2021) 'An evidence review of face masks against COVID-19', *Proceedings of the National Academy of Sciences*, 118(4).

Idle No More (2021) 'We will not celebrate stolen Indigenous land and stolen Indigenous lives. #CANCELCANADADAY', #CancelCanadaDay: No Pride in Genocide. https://idlenomore.ca/cancelcanadaday/

Jackson, M. (2019) 'The connection between white supremacy and colonisation', *E-Tangata*, 24 March. https://e-tangata.co.nz/comment-and-analysis/the-connection-between-white-supremacy/

Kay (2020) 'Against Hate Crime: on resisting the framing of racist attacks as "hate crimes" and refusing complicity with the police', *Daikon*, 26 May. Available at: https://daikon.co.uk/blog/against-hate-crime

Kong, J., Ip, J., Huang, C. and Lin, K. (2021) *A Year of Racist Attacks: Anti-Asian Racism Across Canada One Year into the COVID-19 Pandemic*, Chinese Canadian National Council Toronto Chapter and Fight Covid Racism. https://mcusercontent.com/9fbfd2cf7b2a8256f770fc35c/files/35c9daca-3fd4-46f4-a883-c09b8c12bbca/covidracism_final_report.pdf

Lawrence, B. (2003) 'Gender, race, and the regulation of Native identity in Canada and the United States: An overview', *Hypatia*, 18(2): 3–31.

Lawrence, B. and Dua, E. (2005) 'Decolonizing antiracism', *Social Justice San Francisco*, 32(4): 120–43.

Leung, H. (2020) 'Why wearing a face mask is encouraged in Asia, but shunned in the U.S.', *Time*, 12 March. https://time.com/5799964/coronavirus-face-mask-asia-us/

Madan, G., Wong, E.H.-S. and Chopra, G. (2021) 'Toronto/Tkaronto Mutual Aid Panel', Marvellous Grounds. http://marvellousgrounds.com/blog/toronto-mutual-aid/

Maynard, R. (2017) *Policing Black Lives: State Violence in Canada from Slavery to the Present*. Fernwood Publishing.

Shah, N. (2001) *Contagious Divides: Epidemics and Race in San Francisco's Chinatown*. University of California Press.

Sharpe, C. (2016) *In the Wake: On Blackness and Being*. Duke University Press.

Simpson, L.B. (2017) *As We Have Always Done: Indigenous Freedom Through Radical Resistance*. University of Minnesota Press.

Siu, E. (2020) 'Asian Canadian woman wearing face mask kicked out of Toronto supermarket', *Nextshark*, 18 March. https://nextshark.com/metro-supermarket-asian-woman-face-mask/

Smith, L.T. (2013) *Decolonizing Methodologies: Research and Indigenous Peoples*. Zed Books Ltd.

Sukhdeo, S. (2021) 'Rights not rescue: an interview with Elene Lam, Executive Director of Butterfly', *Ultravires*, 2 May. http://ultravires.ca/2021/05/rights-not-rescue-an-interview-with-elene-lam-executive-director-of-butterfly/

Thobani, S. (2007) *Exalted Subjects: Studies in the Making of Race and Nation in Canada*. University of Toronto Press.

Tsekouras, P. (2020a) ' "It happened because I'm Asian": Toronto ER nurse says she was spit on, verbally assaulted', *CTV News*, 9 April. https://toronto.ctvnews.ca/it-happened-because-i-m-asian-toronto-er-nurse-says-she-was-spit-on-verbally-assaulted-1.4890363

Tsekouras, P. (2020b) ' "We are being singled out": Chinese-Canadian community confronts discrimination amid coronavirus outbreak', *CTV News*, 29 January. https://toronto.ctvnews.ca/we-are-being-singled-out-chinese-canadian-community-confronts-discrimination-amid-coronavirus-outbreak-1.4789011 (Accessed: 7 July 2021).

Walia, H. (2013) *Undoing Border Imperialism*. AK Press.

Wong, E.H.-S. (2020) 'When a disease is racialized', *briarpatch magazine*, 3 February. https://briarpatchmagazine.com/articles/view/when-a-disease-is-racialized-coronavirus-anti-chinese-racism

Yam, K. (2021) 'Viral images show people of color as anti-Asian perpetrators. That misses the big picture', *NBC News*, 15 June. www.nbcnews.com/news/asian-america/viral-images-show-people-color-anti-asian-perpetrators-misses-big-n1270821

Yeung, F. (2020) 'Anti-mask racist rant at T&T'. www.youtube.com/watch?v=ALRZ_01ar40

Young, I. (2020) 'Coronavirus: Asian women in Canada are abused, punched and spat on. Is it racist maskaphobia?', *South China Morning Post*, 12 May. https://sg.news.yahoo.com/coronavirus-asian-women-canada-abused-220836365.html

Yu, H. (2021) 'The white elephant in the room: anti-Asian racism in Canada', *Beyond*. https://beyond.ubc.ca/henry-yu-white-elephant/

ELEVEN

#NoGoingBack: Queer Leaps at the Intersection of Protest and COVID-19[1, 2]

Jin Haritaworn

I write into the snapshot of a world that has gone from frozen to on fire. The police murder of George Floyd has sparked mass protests all over the US and in cities across the West.[3] This is happening during a hypersurveilled pandemic and despite risks of infection and arrest. To a growing critical mass, the fire that is currently lighting up the murderers' headquarters in Minneapolis symbolizes an awareness that state racism is not over. Nor is it irreversible: as we now learn, police forces recently armed with total powers in the name of quarantine can be defunded.

The time we are in has an unhinged feel to it. It is both haunted and prescient (Gordon, 2011). On the one hand, the monster keeps coming back with a new spin – from the virus's ability to shut down all major organs, to the worst recession in centuries, to the children now deemed especially symptomatic. On the other hand, significant change is within reach that even a few weeks ago did not seem possible. At the time of writing, city councils, universities, school boards and unions in Minneapolis and elsewhere are having serious debates whether it is time to dismantle the prison industrial complex, promising to propel us further towards an urban environmental justice that has space for all.

In this article, I resist the pull to snap back into reality and into a normal state, as constantly referenced in politicians' calls to go 'back to normal' and journalists' investigations of the 'new normal'. In this, I follow a demand of the mutual aid movement that is mushrooming around us (for example, Spade, 2020), using both digital and offline methods to step in as markets and states fall apart: #NoGoingBack. As I take the leap to the other side of the pandemic portal, with a body that is marked by both privilege and oppression, I am giving in to the fantastical feel of this era, which we may remember as COVID-19, abolition or yet another forgettable chapter in the racial and colonial Anthropocene (Vergès, 2017). My meditation touches on the ghostly hauntings of institutions that have long upheld our normal but are currently dropping their facades. It proceeds to feel its way into the symbolic and material terrain of the virus, which I envision as a multiracial, multi-species environment. It then surrenders to a dystopic landscape that places the contestation over what is conceivable squarely in the realm of the fantastical (Brown and Imarisha, 2015; Haritaworn et al, 2018). While some of this has taken place digitally, I conclude that the struggle for other realities, which occurs on multiple scales, including inner cities, ancestral territories and queer of colour bodies, is necessarily a multi-method project. In fantasizing our way out of this mess, we have at our disposal a radical collective imagination, fertilized by decades of queer Black, Indigenous and people of colour (BIPOC) art, activism and writing, where the lines between organizing, fiction and speculation are intentionally blurred.[4]

Ghostly architectures

Alongside the noisy mediations, of riots and openings, there is a crumbling, of institutions that have long acted as guardians of how we should live. From the impossibility of getting an appointment at city hall, to the closing of national and regional borders to even the most privileged, the fragile solidarities of nation, Europe and West are fraying. As often when faced with disasters, the neoliberal state is failing, more noticeably now, creating a vacuum for alternative solidarities (Rodriguez et al, 2020).

The traps of the old normal are especially obvious when regarding the necropolitical institutions (Mbembe, 2003), such as police, prisons, reservations, psychiatric institutions, refugee camps and homeless shelters, whose blueprints spread across the globe with that older pandemic, of European expansion. These hauntings loudly accompany the governance of COVID-19.

They start with the racializing logics of quarantine, as evidenced by politicians' attempts to criminalize resistance and stigmatize protesters for supposedly spreading the virus. The civil war declared on Black youth risking their lives during a public health crisis contrasts starkly with the tolerance displayed towards white people wilfully breaking quarantine – from para-militarized vigilantes and libertarians demanding haircuts in the US to German left- and right-wing conspiracy theorists, to white Torontonians picnicking alongside their mayor in the park.

From the start, quarantine has been a racial profiling project, as in the police assault against Ramatoulaye B., a young mother in France buying milk for her baby, allegedly without producing a print-out detailing her trajectory. If, as Foucault (2003) argued, society must be defended, the mechanism of 'protection' – from print-outs to phone apps to immunity passports – repeats the spatial control of colonial pass laws, which hails racialized bodies as always at the wrong place and time. The distinction between the properly alive and the walking dead is executed along familiar lines.

The current wave of police racism has the virus as its sidekick. As protesters spite the risks and take to the streets, the pandemic is weaponized against them. Several have highlighted the targeting of the breath, during an epidemic that shuts down the

lungs and against a Movement for Black Lives whose slogan is
I can't breathe – from active strangulation to teargas and other
cough-inducing chemical warfare, to confining thousands in
prisons where COVID-19 has soared. Belying liberal shock,
abolitionists have long argued that 'it's not police brutality'
(Rodriguez, 2017) – that violence is at the root of a carceral
regime that is not broken but was built this way.

This also holds true for the biopolitical institutions,
often associated with the caring arms of the welfare state.
With the lockdown, the service functions of the state and
the non-profit sector, decimated by neoliberalism, further
dwindled (see, for example, CATIE, 2020). But even as
governments are 're-opening', the institutions designed for
the properly alive, from schools to day care centres, reappear
as health hazards.

Hospitals and nursing homes have become especially shock
worthy as sites of 'premature death' (Gilmore, 2007). Resisting
their fetishistic glorification, hospital workers have drawn
attention to conditions of work and care that foster some for
life while leaving others to die, on both sides of the carer/
cared for divide (Das Gupta, 2020). The deaths of hospital
workers and elders, and the resuscitation of triage from the
medical history books (Ignani et al, 2020), have manifested the
'monster' of neoliberal defunding (Davis, 2020) and clarified
the longevity of a eugenicism that renders non-white lives,
particularly those who are trans and/or disabled, vulnerable
and a priori low priority.

Then there are the forgotten places, now rediscovered as
'corona hotspots', where poor people of colour are reduced
to their labour power, and conditions of working, living and
quarantining already resemble prison: The social housing
blocks. The Amazon, Instacart and Whole Foods warehouses.
The fruit and vegetable farms. The meat plants, where humans
and animals are herded and encamped alongside each other.
The fencing away of these places, through quarantine, zoning
or other means, has long constituted normality.

Across these institutions, the difference between those that safeguard, and those that abandon or take life, is increasingly rhetorical. As everyday acts are resignified as lethal, there is an uncanny doubling of how things appear, widening the chips in the consensus over what is normal. In this gap arises 'a permanent readiness for the Marvelous', as Afrosurrealist Suzanne Césaire once stated (Kelley, 1999).

Fantastical creatures

There is a supernatural feel to the virus. Like most tales of contagion, its setting is non-white (Shah, 2001). From Trump's 'China virus' to Bryan Adams' tirade against 'bat eating, wet market animal selling, virus making greedy bastards', to the huddle of vampire bats on the cover of the left-wing publication *Sopa de Wuhan*, the virus' origin story conjures a demonic, perversely capitalistic Orient (Amadeo, 2020; Beaumont-Thomas, 2020). There, race and species, human and inhuman, modern and premodern inter-breed with impropriety, a trope as old as European racism. The bat features a victim-villain whose vengeance is misplaced onto the 'wrong' humans, who do not inappropriately consume animals or encroach on wildlife. Yet even on the other side of the world, the enlightened 'we' is not safe from the curse, which spreads at the speed of light, or of air travel.

This multi-species narrative of Man and his Others, as Sylvia Wynter calls it (McKittrick, 2015), could only be conceived in a racial Anthropocene. To name racism as the apocalypse is to let go of a universe created by an absolutist deity, be it God or an eco-feminist Earth, whose concept of 'nature' means to inhabit or cohabit with the right/white genders and species. As environmental justice activists have long argued, the fantasy of pristine landscapes freed of humans lends itself to an eco-fascist imaginary (Gosine and Teelucksingh, 2008; Brown, 2020). In this greenwashed variation on white supremacy, nature recovers by ridding itself of humans, but never all equally. In contrast, the ones who show up in the statistics for social and premature death are not the biggest polluters. They are old, sick, poor, disabled, Brown and Black. Their intimacies are criminal, their families too big. Their territories are in the way of 'essential' industries. They are the same ones who have long been deemed disposable.

In the place of this misanthropic universe is a multiplicity of environments that include humans, and cities. Here, catastrophe precedes the apocalyptic event, from melting ice caps to droughts, floods, storms and fires. It precedes disaster capitalism, even. The horror that is 'racial capitalism' (Robinson, 1983), which tops the causes of premature death for Man's Others, is contemporaneous with the violent incorporation of all into modernity.

Marvellous leaps

The dystopic space that is opening up on the crossroads of COVID-19 and protest nevertheless births new possibilities for existing with other human and nonhuman beings. Many are rediscovering the speculative landscapes of Octavia Butler, whose *Parable of the Sower* 1993 is set in a 2020s not unlike our own – one marred by fascist government and abandonment (Brown and Imarisha, 2015). The novel summons the potential for change, a change that is spiritual, and recited as a recurring prayer by its heroine, a multiracial Black woman, and her pod of outcasts, who are literally reaching for the stars. There is a long line of writers like Butler, who encourage us to embrace the fantastical in order to shed the forms that never served us and create space for the purposeful dreaming that is needed to escape the intolerable present.

In taking this current leap, we invite possession by feisty queer ancestors who embraced abnormal and chose connection over isolation. We remember lessons from the Aids crisis – that safer socialities are attractive and that fluidbonded pods are part of a heritage that comforts us in the face of collective devastation. In this legacy, we rediscover quarantining as a methodology of care – of pleasure even.

Our pods, bubbles and care collectives, however officially mis-appropriated, are radical alternatives to state-led lockdown. Our masks are defiant fashion symbols, of ethnic pride, of solidarity, of survivors' genius (Haritaworn, 2020). These subversive performances of quarantine divest from a state-led quarantine regime that deals more death. Their role models are disabled queers of colour (Mingus, 2016). They are disciples of movements for prison abolition and transformative justice, which again seize the moment to create safety and accountability outside of the system. They step into a long legacy of mutual aid by BIPOC looking after each other while the state is nowhere to be found.

As we reject old and new versions of the 'normal', we seize the moment to norm, in whatever medium is available. The digital environments that increasingly absorb our waking energy are full of violence, but they are also populated by repertoires that rehearse other worlds. By visions of uprisings. By acts of solidarity that model possibilities beyond the anti-Blackness that has infected non-Black communities. Like the owners of the Gandhi Mahal restaurant in Minneapolis, damaged during the uprising, whose post affirming that #BlackLivesMatter, by any means necessary, went viral. Or the K-pop fans breaking Dallas Police Department's snitching app with fancam shots of Korean popstars. The TikTok users emptying out Trump's Tulsa rally with fake seat reservations. And the mutual aid groups using digital methods to redistribute real life wealth and practice communication skills in the most unlikely of media, rehearsing communities that are capacious enough to resist fascism.

The two Toronto-based mutual aid groups that inspired my title are not incidentally led by BIPOC women and queers who bring their backgrounds in arts, anti-violence, racial, economic and healing justice, harm reduction and Indigenous feminism. One is called CareMongering, a name that consciously norms for solidarity rather than fearmongering, also reflected in organizers' calls for physical rather than social distancing. The other, (now defunct) Toronto/Tkaronto Mutual Aid is an offshoot of CareMongering and elaborates this vision through a comprehensive set of demands: 'decolonization, healthcare for all, no work obligations, meet basic needs and solidarity not policing', including 'NO to border controls'. Both are on Facebook[5] but broker offline resources, including masks and safety alerts for demonstrators, and engage in struggles impacting offline worlds, such as rent strikes and police defunding.

To recognize the potential of these digital environments for generating spiritual fuel and people power is not to glorify the digital over 'real life'. As digital and media scholars have long shown, the two are inter-connected. There are equal dangers in relying on a digital realm controlled by capital and surveilled by the state, and in eco-fascist yearning for more 'natural' states. We need an urban environmental justice that is neither technophobic nor punitive of those taking back public space. Where we nurture safer ways of leaving the privatized moulds that capitalism has designed for us, as visionary cyborgs or as bodies that engage in the necessary risk of commingling. Where our children grow up loving bats and people and learning to share space as interdependent earthlings. Where our youth teach us how to take down drones and hate pages and grow foods that withstand droughts. As this moment reminds us, our methods must be as queerly expansive as our dreams. They require us to be both safe and promiscuous.

Postscript

The sense of possibility, that large-scale transformation was within reach, was quickly disappointed. To cite Priya Kandaswamy's response to Arundathi Roi, which is fully aware of the problems of the interpellative 'we', if the pandemic opened a portal, we apparently chose not to walk through it (Kandaswamy, 2021). Instead, the dystopias anticipated in Octavia Butler's writing – intensified by the recent escalating climate crisis – have come to further dominate the landscape. The racist and classist government responses to the pandemic that my original article critiqued have if anything become more blatant. While measures taken during the first wave by several governments in Europe, Canada and elsewhere contained some redistributive impulses, states have increasingly pandered to the conspiracy theorists, racists and eugenicists filling our streets. In addition to policing, health care has emerged as a key realm where the lines along which some are prioritized for protection, while others are left to die, have been clarified. My current work discusses this with regard to the German debates over higher rates of infection in migrant and non–white communities, and a vaccination policy that failed to prioritize those who are most vulnerable to the virus (Haritaworn, 2022). Both have constructed racialized people as infectious rulebreakers who do not deserve safety and protection since they always already pose a risk to the properly alive (Haritaworn, 2022). In contrast, I argue that we need to expand and hold space for the abolitionist practices of safety that are currently emerging from marginalized communities that build capacity and provide alternatives for these necropolitical regimes. These include direct challenges to the state, and coalitions to hold the state accountable to redistribute resources, give access to health care, income replacements and other social and economic entitlements, and refrain from racial violence. They also include what I call a transformation of safety, which is in the tradition of community–based alternatives to state violence, a tradition that is abolitionist and indebted to the Black Radical Tradition and Indigenous sovereignty. Examples for this include activist safety protocols that at first sight resemble official hygiene measures – including social distancing, masking, hand sanitizing, decentralized events planning, contact tracing and virtual organizing – but whose radically caring implementation and vision for transformative justice could not be further removed from the carceral relationships that the state and capital seek to mould us into. They further include transformations in the intimate realms of friendship and chosen family that prefigure the world we want to live in. One example for this are the (ongoing) cross-household experiments in pods, bubbles and care collectives that I described earlier, that were re-criminalized during the lockdowns and are directly indebted to queer of colour cultures post-Aids. These lessons, resources and experiences often remain untapped. They teach us that the spaces we manage to hold, however small and temporary, are immensely powerful. They are sites from which larger transformations are being rehearsed all the time. The portal hasn't quite closed yet.

Notes

[1] This chapter originally appeared in the *Journal of Environmental Media*: Haritaworn, J. (2020) '#NoGoingBack: Queer leaps at the intersection of protest and COVID-19', *Journal of Environmental Media*, 1(Supplement): 12.1–12.7, doi: https://doi.org/10.1386/jem_00033_1.

[2] #NoGoingBack was written during the so-called first wave of the coronavirus pandemic, a moment that was at once bleak and lit with possibility. The lockdowns coincided with the biggest global protests against racism of all time, the resurgence of the global movement for Black Lives and the birth of new antiracist movements such as Migrantifa in Germany, a new youth of colour-led organization that rose up in response to the racist killing spree in Hanau on 19 February 2020, that killed 11 and wounded 5, predominantly Muslim, youth. In their protests, public calls and mutual aid projects, Migrantifa clearly name the continuities between fascism, racism and the state. On the conjuncture of pandemic and protest, these injustices that were long eclipsed by neoliberal multiculturalism are being brought to the fore.

The arguments I am making in this reprinted article are part of a larger body of work that makes sense of the close succession of progress narratives involving visible LGBT bodies and spaces as privileged diversity symbols and the coming out of white supremacy and cis-heteropatriarchy as hegemonic regimes that no longer need to be diversified. My book *Queer Lovers and Hateful Others*, for example, examines the figure of the queer lover in late 1990s and 2010s Berlin as a transitional object that helped manufacture consent for policing, gentrification and abandonment, by fettering these practices in the languages of love and care for minorities. COVID-19 marks another such transition.

As white supremacy waxes and neoliberal multiculturalism wanes, who should be left to die so that markets can reopen is made painfully explicit. Yet this is also a moment where visions of transformation are being formulated with increased clarity. The chapter highlights this with the activism of queers who never passed as significant Others, notably queer Black, Indigenous and people of colour (QTBIPOC). In the autonomous spaces of mutual aid and direct action emerging during the pandemic, marvellous grounds appear where alternatives are created and fantastic leaps rehearsed.

[3] George Floyd is not the only Black or Indigenous person who has died at the hands of police. The list of names is overwhelming and includes Tony McDade, Regis Korchinski-Paquet, Chantel Moore, Oury Jalloh and Christy Schwundeck and too many other cis-men, cis-women and transpeople worldwide.

[4] The following thoughts were cross-fertilized by many. I have been inspired by the words and actions of many fellow queer/BIPOC/migrant activist scholars during this time, such as Paola Bacchetta, Gunjan Chopra, Kusha Dadui, Sedina Fiati, Audrey Huntley, Ren-Yo Hwang, Andrew Jolivette, Adi Kuntsman, Margo Okazawa-Rey, Ana Clarisa Rojas Durazo, Amita Swadhin and Vanessa Thompson.

[5] Previously available at www.facebook.com/groups/TO.Community. Response.COVID19/ (accessed in 2021) and currently at www. facebook.com/mutual.aid.TO (accessed 7 June 2022). Digital archives are ephemeral and frequently disappear for a variety of reasons, including activist burnout, changes in the historical context, and the capitalist principle underlying many social media.

References

Amadeo, P. (2020) 'Sopa de Wuhan: Pensamiento contemporáneo en tiempos de Pandemias', *ASPO* (*Aislamiento Social Preventivo y Obligatorio*). www.elextremosur.com/nota/23685-sopa-dewu han-el-libro-completo-y-gratis-para-leer-sobre-el-coronavirus/

Beaumont-Thomas, B. (2020) 'Bryan Adams attacks China as "bat-eating, virus-making" source', *The Guardian*, 12 May. www.theg uardian.com/music/2020/may/12/bryan-adams-attacks-china-coronavirus.

Brown, A.M. and Imarisha, W. (eds) (2015) *Octavia's Brood: Science Fiction Stories from Social Justice Movements*, AK Press.

Brown, S. (2020) 'Humans are not the virus', *Wear Your Voice Magazine*, 23 March. https://wearyourvoicemag.com/humans-are-not-the-viruseco-fascist/

Butler, O. (1993) *Parable of the Sower*. Four Walls Eight Windows.

CATIE (2020) 'Coping with COVID-19: Insight from the front lines of HIV, hepatitis C and harm reduction', 26 March. www.catie.ca/en/webinars/coping-covid-19-insight-front-lines-hiv-hepatitis-c-and-harmreduction

Das Gupta, T. (2020) 'Inquiry into coronavirus nursing home deaths needs to include discussion of workers and race', *The Conversation*, 26 May. https://theconversation.com/inquiry-into-coronavirus-nursing-home-deathsneeds-to-include-discussion-of-workers-and-race-139017

Davis, M. (2020) 'COVID-19: The monster is finally at the door', *MR Online*, 19 March. https://mronline.org/2020/03/19/mike-davis-on-covid-19-themonster-is-finally-at-the-door/

Foucault, M. (2003) *Society Must Be Defended*, Macmillan.

Gilmore, R.W. (2007) *Golden Gulag: Prisons, Surplus, Crisis, and Opposition in Globalizing*, University of California Press.

Gordon, A. (2011) 'Some thoughts on haunting and futurity', *Borderlands*, 10(2): 1–21.

Gosine, A. and Teelucksingh, C. (2008) *Environmental Racism in Canada*, Emond Montgomery.

Haritaworn, J. (2020) '#NoGoingBack #NobodyLeftBehind: Leaping into marvellous grounds', online lecture. www.xartsplitta.net/en/notgoingback-nobodyleftbehind/

Haritaworn, J. (2022) 'Riskante Migrant*innen und schützenswerte Bürger*innen: Die Transformation der Sicherheit in der Konjunktur von Pandemie und Protest' (Risky migrants and citizens worthy of protection: The transformation of safety on the conjuncture of pandemic and protest), in D. Loick and V.E. Thompson (eds), *Behemoth. Abolitionist Futures: Prefigurations Beyond Violence*, 14(3): 25–46.

Haritaworn, J., Moussa, G. and Ware, S.M. (eds) (2018) *Marvellous Grounds: Queer of Colour Histories of Toronto*, Between The Lines.

Ignani, E., Chandler, E. and Erickson, L. (2020) 'Crips and COVID in Canada', *iHuman*. http://ihuman.group.shef.ac.uk/crips-and-covid-in-canada

Kandaswamy, P. (2021) Facebook update. No link available, cited with permission of the author.

Kelley, R.G. (1999) 'A poetics of anticolonialism', *MR Zine*, 1 November. https://monthlyreview.org/1999/11/01/a-poetics-of-anticolonialism

Mbembe, A. (2003) 'Necropolitics', *Public Culture*, 15(1): 11–40.

McKittrick, K. (ed.) (2015) *Sylvia Wynter: On Being Human as Praxis*, Duke University Press.

Mingus, M. (2016) 'Pods and pod making worksheet', June. https://batjc.wordpress.com/pods-and-pod-mapping-worksheet

Oxfam (2022) 'Ten richest men double their fortunes in pandemic while incomes of 99 percent of humanity fall', Oxfam.org, January. www.oxfam.org/en/press-releases/ten-richest-men-double-their-fortunes-pandemic-while-incomes-99-percent-humanity

Robinson, C. (1983) *Black Marxism: The Making of the Black Radical Tradition*, Zed Books.

Rodriguez, D. (2017) 'It's not police brutality', *YouTube*, 13 September. www.youtube.com/watch?v=ylEUT2BvvtM

Rodriguez, D., Gilmer, R., Peña, H., Henderson, A., Tendaji Ujimaa, A., Kaba, M. and Spade, D. (2020) ' "Mutual aid" is a people's movement', ASA teach-in, YouTube, 4 May. www.youtube.com/watch?v=pZwz7IG_I9U

Shah, N. (2001) *Contagious Divides: Epidemics and Race in San Francisco's Chinatown*, University of California Press.

Spade, D. (2020) 'Solidarity not charity', *Social Text*, 38(1): 131–51.

Verges, F. (2017) 'Racial Capitalocene', in G.T. Johnson and A. Lubin (eds), *Futures of Black Radicalism* (pp 72–82), Verso.

TWELVE

Conclusion

Sunera Thobani

At the time of writing, Trump-inspired anti-vaxxers and related white supremacist organizations have occupied Canada's capital, Ottawa, bringing to a standstill the country's biggest border with the US. Similar actions are being organized in the US and Europe. Meanwhile, Oxfam (2022) reports the ten richest men in the world – all white – doubled their wealth during the first years of the pandemic. Governments are lifting pandemic measures, including mask mandates, vaccination requirements, and self-isolation for positive cases, even as COVID-19 continues to mutate. Publicly funded testing is ending, as is data collection on positive cases. Minimizing the pandemic is the main strategy as governments offload onto individuals the burden to protect their own health. Can such abdication of state responsibility for *public* health in an ongoing *global* crisis yield other than greater devastation?

Our book shows how COVID-19 exposed yet again the failures of a profit-driven system even now fixated on deregulation, privatization and rampant consumerism. What passes as economic advancement is cannabalizing the social order, and has made the planet unsustainable. This is abundantly clear every day, everywhere. Concentrating wealth and power among a small elite that is profiting handsomely from the pandemic, the Western state-form condemns millions to illness, destitution and premature death.

COVID-19's interaction with racialization, coloniality and underdevelopment is identified here as heightening processes of dispossession and disenfranchisement to deadly effects. We have shown how the liberal valorization of inclusion leads to a vacuous 'decoloniality', how a return to the pre-pandemic 'normal' will only entrench deeper the confluence of environmental devastation, imperialist war and mass migration to produce ever new crises. We also question the over-reliance on vaccines as the way out of this crisis. Indeed, control of the vaccine itself has created an apartheid that condemns millions to early death or the debilitations of 'long COVID'. Access to vaccination is clearly vital, but this can only be effective as part of a multi-pronged, holistic approach that requires, at the very minimum, accountable and equitable distribution, transparent and ethical governance.

No doubt official commissions and inquiries will be appointed in many of our research sites to examine the failures of public health measures. Throughout this pandemic, numerous well considered policy recommendations have been made from many quarters. These include maintaining public health measures; lifting intellectual property rights on vaccines; and increasing access to healthcare, food, housing, water and income security. There is little need for us to rehearse these recommendations here, it is more than obvious that prioritization of at-risk populations, in the Global South and North, is an urgent necessity. Our contribution to this discussion underscores the indispensibility of responsible and accountable collective action, committed to the realization of justice in the international order. The pandemic is global, so too must be its countermeasures. To this end, the overarching recommendation arising from our research is that public health measures be based upon, and advance, three main principles: justice, reparations and reconstruction. Our vision for justice is global, it includes economic as well as political justice, juridical as well as social. This conception of justice requires an end to the colonial and racial exploitations that grease the wheels of the global economy.

Moreover, although reparations are not an ultimate solution, no reconstruction of life-enhancing values, practices and relations is possible in their absence. These three principles – justice, reparations, reconstruction – require immediately, at a minimum, the following actions:

- global distribution of vaccines, prioritizing those countries and communities with the lowest level of access;
- ending intellectual property rights to share vaccine, and eventually all, scientific and medical technologies, as well as their production and distribution;
- publicly funded mass testing, as well as universal access to health care, income and employment support, safe housing, clean water and food;
- access to sanctuary, social services, rights and supports for migrants, refugees, and the undocumented; and
- mass health education campaigns led by grassroots level, collective, community leadership.

No doubt these measures are reformist, but they are vital to ending the global pandemic. They can be funded by a globally enforced progressive taxation system, directed especially at the corporate sector. The enactment of these measures will further the large-scale reorganization of global and national economies and polities on the basis of transparency and accountability.

Contemporary anti-racist and anti-colonial organizing, including the anti-Islamophobia and anti-war movements, the Indigenous Resurgence and Black Lives Matter movements, have gained significant momentum and public support. Building a politics of solidarity among them on the recognition that colonialism and its racial hierarchies constitute a global structure of power that advances westerity and white imperialist supremacy would make for an unstoppable revolutionary force for radical economic-political transformation.

Given the failures of the most powerful nation-states to avert the pandemic, and given their investment in corporate driven privatization, the path to sustainable futures lies only in collective action to transform their life-destroying practices and divide-and-rule technologies of governance. Social movements, community organizations, trusted community leaders, families and individuals are even now advancing practices of care, collective responsibility and accountability. It is in these networks of interdependence, trust and solidarity that possibilities open up for sustainable, even miraculous, futures.

Index

Page numbers in **bold** refer to tables and those in *italic* refer to figures in the text.